IN PRAISE

of

LABS

IN PRAISE
of

LABS

An Illustrated Treasury

Edited by John Yow

SMITHMARK

Design & Compilation © 1999 Lionheart Books, Ltd.
All images licensed by Applejack Licensing International
of Manchester, Vermont 05255, (802) 362-3662.
All artwork Copyrighted to the individual artists:
Kevin Daniel © 6, 11, 20, 24, 29, 30, 33, 37, 38, 41, 44, 47, 52, 59, 62, 69, 70, 78, 80,
92, 96, 97, 99, 100, 109, 114, 121, 123, 124, 131, 136, 148
Nigel Hemming © 1, 3, 7, 8, 10, 12, 13, 14, 18, 21, 34, 42, 45, 51, 53, 54, 55, 56, 58,
60, 64, 66, 71, 74, 77, 79, 82, 85, 88, 89, 91, 93, 101, 102, 104, 107, 116, 118, 120,
125, 130, 133, 140, 143, 147, 152, 153, 156, 158, 159
Michael Jackson © 110, 151
John Silver © 9, 31, 39, 65, 94, 113, 137
Joseph Sulkowski © 103

This edition published in 1999 by SMITHMARK Publishers,
a division of U.S. Media Holdings, Inc., 115 West 18th Street,
New York, NY 10011.

SMITHMARK books are available for bulk purchase for sales promotion
and premium use. For details write or call the manager of special sales,
SMITHMARK Publishers,
115 West 18th Street, New York, NY 10011, (212) 519-1300.

In Praise of Labs
was produced by Lionheart Books, Ltd.,
5105 Peachtree Industrial Blvd., Atlanta, Georgia 30341

Design: Carley Wilson Brown
Cover Art: Nigel Hemming, "The New Recruit"

ISBN: 0-7651-1665-0

Printed in Hong Kong

10 9 8 7 6 5 4 3 2 1

Library of Congress Cataloging-in-Publication Data

In praise of Labs : an illustrated treasury / edited by John Yow.
    p.   cm.
ISBN 0-7651-1665-0 (hardcover)
    1. Labrador retriever--Anecdotes. 2. Labrador retriever-
-Pictorial works.   I. Yow, John Sibley, 1948-   .
SF429.L315   1999
636.752'7--dc21   98-55572
                                                                CIP

Table of Contents

The Little Newfoundler

By The Earl of Malmesbury

England

The Little Newfoundler (dog) was imported into England in either 1823 or 1824 by the second Earl of Malmesbury, my great, great grandfather, born August 1798. As a young man, he was one of Pitt's bright young men, and was a Junior Minister for Foreign Affairs and MP for both Helston and Heytesbury. After the Battle of Copenhagen, when he was responsible for the Danish minister, whom he was authorized to assure that no battle would take place, he (the then Viscount FitzHarris) came out of politics.

6

"Family Portrait" ~ Nigel Hemming

"Recollect that the Almighty, who gave the dog to be companion of our pleasures and our toils,

hath invested him with a nature noble and incapable of deceit."

—Sir Walter Scott

At about this time, he inherited the Manor House and Estate of Hurn, near Christchurch, from a first cousin, Mr. Edward Hooper, who had been chairman of customs and excise. On leaving the political field, Pitt made him governor of the Isle of Wight. The Isle of Wight was then strategically important—the French, ready for invasion, were only just across the Channel.

In 1815, his beloved wife, Harriet, suddenly died in great agony—caused, the family thought, by a burst appendix. He was a bereft widower and a very lonely man, left with three young boys, the eldest of whom was only nine years old— later to become Secretary of State for Foreign Affairs and Lord Keeper of the Privy Seal. The second son later became Admiral Sir Edward Harris, and the youngest bishop of Gibraltar. The second earl became a leading ornithologist, and is still quoted today.

Bournemouth at that time consisted of only six fisherman's cottages, nestling on the mouth of the tiny River Bourne. Not far away—to the east—was Christchurch and its two rivers, the Avon and the Stour, with their vast areas of marshland—the home and breeding ground of innumerable species of wild fowl.

This preamble is written so that one can understand how the personality and character of the Little Newfoundler fit into my great, great grandfather's lonely life.

The Newfoundland fishing fleet, with its load of cod and other fish kept on ice in the hold, came regularly into Poole Harbour, which was not all that far to the west of Hurn. After the fish had been sold, the ice was bought by the local squires, who kept it in what is known as their ice houses, which were holes dug into the ground some twelve feet or so, lined with brick, with a brick dome roof covered with topsoil and grass, which was encouraged to grow all over the dome. Trees, mainly oak, were planted alongside to give increased cover and shade. Under these conditions, the ice kept well. They were fascinating buildings. On our Hurn estate there were two, and one is still in reasonable condition, with its two-and-a-half-inch thick oak double doors.

These ice houses were hazardous if the doors were not kept shut, for there were cattle grazing nearby. Cattle, like most animals, are inquisitive. I remember well a cow falling in. The question was—how could the cow be gotten out alive? We did it by persuading her to climb up straw bales which we had piled in. I have digressed!

It was usual for each ship to carry at least one dog on board. My great, great grandfather on occasions rode over to Poole Harbour and saw these dogs playing in the sea, retrieving the fish that had not been kept and had been thrown out. He thought himself that these water dogs, who retrieved so naturally in the water, were exactly what he required for his wildfowling. He acquired two couples and built kennels on high

"Country Companions" ~ John Silver

ground for them, near a bend of the River Stour, known as Blackwater, which was only a quarter of a mile above the official tide end of the river. He bred from these dogs. I remember these kennels well. They have since been pulled down. Improved kennels have been built some little distance away by a newer house, where the keeper lived in a wood, with the fascinating name of Quomp Copse, pronounced "Coombe."

At about this time, the then Duke of Buccleugh imported, also from another Newfoundland fishing fleet which sailed into the River Clyde in Scotland, a couple of Little Newfoundlers. Unfortunately, this strain died out almost at once—so we gave them a pair, descended from our own imported dogs.

When our keeper, Mr. Beech, was called up during the First World War, in the Royal Artillery, the bitch he left behind pined so much she sadly died. I just remember her as a child. She was the last of the direct descendants of the dogs imported in 1823.

It was the third Earl of Malmesbury who changed the name from the Little Newfoundlers to the appropriate name of Labrador. He felt the "Little Newfoundler" was too much of a mouthful. Needless to say, my family have had Labradors ever since, but sadly not the immediate direct strain.

One had always appreciated that the Labrador had derived its retrieving instinct from retrieving fish, but I had never seen a dog actually doing this. From time immemorial, Hurn had always suffered from severe flooding from the River Stour. On one occasion, the floods were receding and it seemed a good time to go out wildfowling. I was about sixteen at this time, and took my gun and Labrador onto the Meads, which were crossed by large ditches. Fish, after a flood, were frequently stranded in these ditches. I shot a left and right at two pike. I wondered if my dog would retrieve them. He went into the water without hesitation—they weighed twelve and ten pounds, respectively.

Our dogs always slept in our bedrooms. I never accepted the fact that dogs had to be banished to some kennel at night. I realized from my earliest days that they should be with one as much as possible. Conversations and so-called discussions and games enabled dog and master to thoroughly understand each other—important factors when at work on a difficult retrieve!—at times the dog would know more than its master, and, of course, vice versa. A good retrieve involved team work.

I remember one particular occasion not so long ago. I was not carrying a gun, but only picking up. One of the guns had a young and rather wild dog which "ran in" continuously. We were in a large oak and coppice wood. The young dog had run in on one or two occasions, much to the displeasure of my dog, who had been restrained in the early part of the pheasant drive. A wounded bird and a strong runner appeared, and I was ordered to go after it. The young dog was running wild. My dog caught him, got hold of one of his hind legs, tipped him up and held him down, squealing, for a short time, as if to say, "That will teach you!" When my dog let him go, he returned to his master; I heard the master say severely to him, "That will teach you a lesson." Meanwhile, my dog disappeared for what must have been all of five minutes and returned to me with the wounded bird in his mouth and a smile on his face—delighted with himself! I had to tell him he'd been very clever.

Continuing the yarning—Lord Dorchester, my father-in-law, had a dog he was very fond of, and the dog was very fond of him. Sometimes they had a difference of opinion as to the direction of the bird. My father-in-law was not a particularly patient man, and scents had been difficult that morning. At lunch, everyone came in and huddled round a fire. My father-in-law was startled to hear a little girl saying to her mother, "Lord Dorchester's dog has a funny name, hasn't he?" "What name was that?" asked her mother. The answer came "Damn you Dexter!"

The versatility of the Labrador cannot be overemphasized. There was a dog at Hurn with a dual role, guarding the estate workshop. He would allow those menacing characters who would come in to "borrow" tools to enter, and frequently not allow them to leave if they had a tool in their hand. This dog was also an excellent water dog.

I could not resist writing these personal tales and anecdotes. I end with those superb lines from "Alice Through the Looking Glass"—

"The time has come, the walrus said
To talk of many things,
Of shoes, and ships, and sealing wax,
And cabbages and kings,
And why the sea is boiling hot
And whether pigs have wings."

Reprinted from

THE LABRADOR QUARTERLY ~ 1994

The XVth Day

By Gene Hill

"And God created the heavens, and the earth,

and the Labrador thereof."

On the fifteenth day, or thereabouts, God and the Recording Angel were just taking it easy. Spread out beneath them was *The Creation*, and despite last-minute changes, they were feeling rather smug with the way it had all gone: so many miracles sound easier than they really are.

God was especially interested in Adam and Eve. He considered them the centerpiece of the whole scheme, and as he watched them, he got the feeling something was a bit off.

"Taking A Breather" ~ Nigel Hemming

Eve had taken to spending more and more time sitting and staring at herself in one of the pools, fussing with her hair and trying to decide which was her best side. Adam was throwing sticks in the brook and watching them sail away. As God and the Recording Angel watched, Adam threw another stick, walked over to where Eve was working on a braid, and shouted. "Back!", pointing at the stick with his finger. Eve barely gave him a glance as she stuck a large red flower in her hair, and continued to stare into the pool.

The Recording Angel finally broke the silence. "Lord," he said, "something's missing."

"I know," God said, "but I can't quite put my finger on it."

Adam was still standing close to Eve and watching another stick he'd thrown. This time they heard him say, "Back Eve!" As they watched, Eve slowly got up, waded out into the water, and brought back the stick. Just as God was about to smile, Eve swung the stick and broke it against Adam's shin.

"I think he needs a creature that will

play with him," God said. He made a quick motion with his forefinger, and the stick that was lying across Adam's foot suddenly became a snake. Adam looked at it for a moment and then got another stick, waved it in front of the snake, threw it a few feet into the water, and shouted, "Back!" The snake looked at Adam in a curious way, then slithered over to where Eve sat and whispered something in her ear. Eve looked up at Adam and made a small circular motion with her finger at her temple. The snake seemed to nod in agreement, and the two of them went off together, leaving Adam standing alone by the edge of the water.

"It's not the right size or something," the Recording Angel said. "It ought to be bigger."

"I've got just the right thing," God answered. The rock that Eve had been sitting on suddenly stood up and yawned, showing great shining ivory teeth. God smiled.

"What's that?" the Recording Angel asked.

"Hippo," He said, obviously pleased with Himself.

Adam could see that the hippo enjoyed being in the water. He got another stick, larger than the one he'd thrown for the snake. The stick made a great splash and Adam watched expectantly as the giant beast slid into the water and disappeared. After almost an hour and no sign of the hippo, except an occasional water spout, Adam sat down on the bank and cradled his head in his arms. He was still sitting there in the fading light when Eve returned with the snake at her side. She was carrying a handful of leaves, which she tried on, looking for Adam's approval. He finally pointed at one she'd discarded and she angrily tore it in half and tossed it in the pool.

"Eve's acting a little cross, Lord," the Angel remarked.

"Well, nobody's perfect," God answered, somewhat annoyed.

It was getting dark when God turned to the Recording Angel and said, "I'm going to hold up the night for a while until we get this thing solved. What's left on inventory for delivery?"

The Recording Angel hauled out a thick scroll and began reading out loud, starting with *aardvark*. God listened attentively but did nothing more than occasionally shake His head, now and then making an outline of something in the earth with the quill-end of a long white feather. At the end of the list, the Recording Angel waited fretfully for God to ask him what a *zygote* was, but He didn't. The Angel was quite relieved; so much of the small stuff tended to look alike.

Suddenly God smiled. "I think I've got it," He said, waving His hand at a small passing cloud, which stopped and rained on the ground where He had been sketching. God began taking handfuls of mud and shaped them this way and that. As He worked, He spoke aloud, as if to give the Recording Angel a lesson in creating.

"It's got to just the right size; strong, but not so big it's always knocking things over," He said. "It ought to like the water about as much as the land, so we'll give it a nice thick coat and a powerful tail—and even webbed feet!"

"You're not making another duck, are you?" the Recording Angel asked, somewhat anxiously. He knew God loved ducks, but He'd made so many already that it was difficult to tell them apart.

"No, nothing like that at all. This creature has four legs and can't fly. The really important thing is the disposition. I don't want it to ever get cross with Adam. I want it to follow him around and be good company, to please Adam more than anything else. If Adam wants to run, it will run with him; if Adam want to play, it will play with him."

God paused for a moment and then said, "I thought Eve would be like that, but maybe I used a little too much rib."

He continued to work with the clay, broadening the head and chest, shaping the leg and tail until they were just so. He looked it over with great care, and then said in a deep and warm voice that more than hinted at His pleasure, "That's good."

The Recording Angel walked around behind Him. "I really like the looks of it, Lord," he said. "What are you going to call it?"

The Lord smiled and said, "A Labrador retriever."

"Won't that be a little hard for Adam to spell?"

"No," He said, "all he has to remember is *i* before *e*."

Then he reached out and touched the clay and said, "Sit." The glossy black hair rippled over the heavy muscles as the Labrador sat, brown eyes sparkling merrily. He seemed to be begging to be asked to do something. God reached for the Recording Angel's staff, broke off a foot or so, and threw it. Then the Lord said, "Back!"

Instantly, the Labrador broke into a full-speed run, tumbled head-over-heels as he grabbed the stick, and brought it back. God threw it again, and the Labrador bounded off even more joyously. When he came back, God and the Recording Angel were grinning like schoolboys.

"Let me try it!" the Recording Angel asked, and threw the stick far across a distant stream. The Labrador leaped into the water, and, almost before they could believe it, was back in front of them, quivering with happiness.

The next day, the Recording Angel and God watched for most of the morning as Adam threw stick after stick and his retriever, seemingly tireless, ran and swam and brought them back with an almost palpable joy. Eve stood off to one side watching them. Finally, she walked over, picked up a stick and threw it. The Labrador sat, watching. When she cried, "Back," he leaped into the air and almost flew into the water. Eve laughed as the droplets wet her. When he returned and gave her the stick, she took it and playfully tugged at his ear. The Labrador raised his head and licked her hand. God and the Recording Angel watched her smile; it was radiant in its loveliness.

"I think I'll make one for Eve," God said.

"Exactly the same?" asked the Recording Angel.

"Yes and no," God replied.

The Recording Angel had made his staff whole again and stood leaning on it for the longest while. Then in a very quiet voice, he said, "Lord, would it be too much to ask you to make one more? Then we could keep it here just to make sure it's perfect."

The Lord smiled and said, "I was thinking the very same thing."

Reprinted from

FIELD & STREAM ~ 1986

"He knew his lord—he knew and strove to meet.

In vain he strove to crawl, and kiss his feet;

Yet (all he could) his tail, his ears, his eyes,

Salute his master and confess his joys.

Soft pity touch'd the mighty master's soul,

Adown his cheek a tear unbidden stole.

The dog whom Fate had granted to behold

His lord, when twenty tedious years had roll'd,

Takes a last look, and having seen him dies;

So closed forever faithful Argus' eyes."

—HOMER, *The Odyssey*

"No man can be condemned for owning a dog. As long as he has a dog, he has a friend;

"Seven Up" ~ Nigel Hemming

and the poorer he gets, the better friend he has."—WILL ROGERS

The Dustbin Dog

By James Herriot

In the semi-darkness of the surgery passage I thought it was a hideous growth dangling from the side of the dog's face, but as he came closer I saw that it was only a condensed milk can. Not that condensed milk cans are commonly found sprouting from dogs' cheeks, but I was relieved because I knew I was dealing with Brandy again.

I hoisted him on to the table. "Brandy, you've been at the dustbin again."

The big golden Labrador gave me an apologetic grin and did his best to lick my face. He couldn't manage it since his tongue was jammed inside the can, but he made up for it by a furious wagging of tail and rear end.

"Patience" ~ Nigel Hemming

"A dog is like an eternal Peter Pan,

a child who never grows old and who therefore

is always available to love and be loved."

—AARON HATCHER

"Oh, Mr. Herriot, I am sorry to trouble you again." Mrs. Westby, his attractive young mistress, smiled ruefully. "He just won't keep out of that dustbin. Sometimes the children and I can get the cans off ourselves but this one is stuck fast. His tongue is trapped under the lid."

"Yes . . . yes . . . I eased my finger along the jagged edge of the metal. "It's a bit tricky, isn't it? We don't want to cut his mouth."

As I reached for a pair of forceps I thought of the many other occasions when I had done something like this for Brandy. He was one of my patients, a huge, lolloping, slightly goofy animal, but this dustbin raiding was becoming an obsession.

He liked to fish out a can and lick out the tasty remnants, but his licking was carried out with such dedication that he burrowed deeper and deeper until he got stuck. Again and again he had been freed by his family or myself from fruit salad cans, corned beef cans, baked bean cans, soup cans. There didn't seem to be any kind of can he didn't like.

I gripped the edge of the lid with my forceps and gently bent it back along its length till I was able to lift it away from the tongue. An instant later, that tongue was slobbering all over my cheek as Brandy expressed his delight and thanks.

"Get back, you daft dog!" I said, laughing, as I held the panting face away from me.

"Yes, come down, Brandy." Mrs. Westby hauled him from the table and spoke sharply. "It's all very fine making a fuss now, but you're becoming a nuisance with this business. It will have to stop."

The scolding had no effect on the lashing tail and I saw that his mistress was smiling. You just couldn't help liking Brandy, because he was a great ball of affection and tolerance without an ounce of malice in him.

I had seen the Westby children—there were three girls and a boy—carrying him around by the legs, upside down, or pushing him in a pram, sometimes dressed in baby clothes. Those youngsters played all sorts of games with him, but he suffered them all with good humour. In fact I am sure he enjoyed them.

Brandy had other idiosyncrasies apart from his fondness for dustbins. I was attending the Westby cat at their home one afternoon when I noticed the dog acting strangely. Mrs. Westby was sitting knitting in an armchair while the oldest girl squatted on the hearth rug with me and held the cat's head.

It was when I was searching my pockets for my thermometer that I noticed Brandy slinking into the room. He wore a furtive air as he moved across the carpet and sat down with studied carelessness in front of his mistress. After a few moments he began to work his rear end gradually up the front of the chair towards her knees. Absently she took a hand away from her knitting and pushed him down, but he immediately restarted his backward ascent. It was an extraordinary mode of progression, his hips moving in a very slow rumba rhythm as he elevated them inch by inch, and all the time the golden face was blank and innocent as though nothing at all was happening.

Fascinated, I stopped hunting for my thermometer and watched. Mrs. Westby was absorbed in an intricate part of her knitting and didn't seem to notice that Brandy's bottom was now firmly parked on her shapely knees which were clad in blue jeans. The dog paused as though acknowledging that phase one had been successfully completed, then ever so gently he began to consolidate his position, pushing his way up the front of the chair with his fore limbs till at one time he was almost standing on his head.

It was at that moment, just when one final backward heave would have seen the great dog ensconced on her lap, that Mrs. Westby finished the tricky bit of knitting and looked up.

"Oh, really, Brandy, you are silly!" She put a hand on his rump and sent him slithering disconsolately to the carpet where he lay and looked at her with liquid eyes.

"What was all that about?" I asked.

Mrs. Westby laughed. "Oh, it's these old blue jeans. When Brandy first came here as a tiny puppy I spent hours nursing him on my knee and I used to wear the jeans a lot then. Ever since, even though he's a grown dog, the very sight of the things makes him try to get on my knee."

> . . . then ever so gently he began to consolidate his position, pushing his way up the front of the chair with his fore limbs till at one time he was almost standing on his head.

"But he doesn't just jump up?"

"Oh no," she said. "He's tried it and got ticked off. He knows perfectly well I can't have a huge Labrador in my lap."

"So now it's the stealthy approach, eh?"

She giggled. "That's right. When I'm preoccupied—knitting or reading—sometimes he manages to get nearly all the way up, and if he's been playing in the mud he makes an awful mess and I have to go and change. That's when he really does receive a scolding."

A patient like Brandy added colour to my daily round. When I was walking my own dog I often saw him playing in the fields by the river. One particularly hot day, many of the dogs were taking to the water either to chase sticks or just to cool off, but whereas they glided in and swam off sedately, Brandy's approach was unique.

I watched as he ran up to the river bank, expecting him to pause before entering. But instead he launched himself outwards, legs splayed in a sort of swallow dive, and hung for a moment in the air rather like a flying fox before splashing thunderously into the depths. To me it was the action of a completely happy extrovert.

On the following day in those same

fields I witnessed something even more extraordinary. There is a little children's playground in one corner—a few swings, a roundabout and a slide. Brandy was disporting himself on the slide.

For this activity he had assumed an uncharacteristic gravity of expression and stood calmly in the queue of children. When his turn came he mounted the steps, slid down the metal slope, all dignity and importance, then took a staid walk round to rejoin the queue.

The little boys and girls who were his companions seemed to take him for granted, but I found it difficult to tear myself away. I could have watched him all day.

I often smiled to myself when I thought of Brandy's antics, but I didn't smile when Mrs. Westby brought him into the surgery a few months later. His bounding ebullience had disappeared and he dragged himself along the passage to the consulting-room.

As I lifted him on to the table I noticed that he had lost a lot of weight.

"Now, what is the trouble, Mrs. Westby?" I asked.

She looked at me worriedly. "He's been off colour for a few days now, listless and coughing and not eating very well, but this morning he seems quite ill and you can see he's starting to pant."

"Yes . . . yes . . ." As I inserted the thermometer I watched the rapid rise and fall of the rib cage and noted the gaping mouth and anxious eyes. "He does look very sorry for himself."

His temperature was 104°F. I took out my stethoscope and auscultated his lungs. I have heard of an old Scottish doctor describing a seriously ill patient's chest as sounding like a 'kist o' whustles' and that just about described Brandy's. Rales, wheezes, squeaks and bubblings—they were all there against a background of laboured respiration.

I put the stethoscope back in my pocket. "He's got pneumonia."

"Oh dear." Mrs. Westby reached out and touched the heaving chest. "That's bad, isn't it?"

"Yes, I'm afraid so."

"But. . ." She gave me an appealing glance. "I understand it isn't so fatal since the new drugs came out."

I hesitated. "Yes, that's quite right. In humans and most animals the sulpha drugs and now penicillin have changed the picture completely, but dogs are still very difficult to cure."

Thirty years later it is still the same. Even with all the armoury of antibiotics which followed penicillin—streptomycin, the tetracyclines, and synthetics, and the new non-antibiotic drugs and steroids—I still hate to see pneumonia in a dog.

"But you don't think it's hopeless?" Mrs. Westby asked.

"No, no, not at all. I'm just warning you that so many dogs don't respond to treatment when they should. But Brandy is young and strong. He must stand a fair chance. I wonder what started this off, anyway."

"Oh, I think I know, Mr. Herriot. He had a swim in the river about a week ago. I try to keep him out of the water in this cold weather but if he sees a stick floating he just takes a dive into the middle. You've seen him—it's one of the funny little things he does."

"Yes, I know. And was he shivery afterwards?"

"He was. I walked him straight home, but it was such a freezing cold day. I could feel him trembling as I dried him down."

I nodded. "That would be the cause, all right. Anyway, let's start his treatment. I'm going to give him this injection of penicillin and I'll call at your house tomorrow to repeat it. He's not well enough to come to the surgery."

"Very well, Mr. Herriot. And is there anything else?"

"Yes, there is. I want you to make him what we call a pneumonia jacket. Cut two holes in an old blanket for his forelegs and stitch him into it along his back. You can use an old sweater if you like, but he must have his chest warmly covered. Only let him out in the garden for necessities."

I called and repeated the injection on the following day. There wasn't much change. I injected him for four more days and the realisation came to me sadly that Brandy was like so many of the others—he wasn't responding. The temperature did drop a little but he hardly ate anything and grew gradually thinner. I put him on sulphapyridine tablets, but they didn't seem to make any difference.

As the days passed and he continued to cough and pant and to sink deeper into a blank-eyed lethargy, I was forced more and more to a conclusion which, a few weeks ago, would have seemed impossible: that this happy, bounding animal was going to die.

But Brandy didn't die. He survived. You couldn't put it any higher than that. His temperature came down and his appetite improved and he climbed on to a plateau of twilight existence where he seemed content to stay.

"He isn't Brandy any more," Mrs. Westby said one morning a few weeks later when I called in. Her eyes filled with tears as she spoke.

I shook my head. "No, I'm afraid he isn't. Are you giving him the halibut-liver oil?"

"Yes, every day. But nothing seems to do him any good. Why is he like this, Mr. Herriot?"

"Well, he has recovered from a really virulent pneumonia, but it's left him with a chronic pleurisy, adhesions and probably other kinds of lung damage. It looks as though he's just stuck there."

She dabbed at her eyes. "It breaks my heart to see him like this. He's only five, but he's like an old, old dog. He was so full of life, too." She sniffed and blew her nose. "When I think of how I used to scold him for getting into the dustbins and muddying up my jeans. How I wish he would do some of his funny old tricks now."

I thrust my hands deep into my pockets. "Never does anything like that now, eh?"

"No, no, just hangs about the house. Doesn't even want to go for a walk."

As I watched, Brandy rose from his place in the corner and pottered slowly over to the fire. He stood there for a moment, gaunt and dead-eyed, and he seemed to notice me for the first time because the end of his tail gave a brief twitch before he coughed, groaned and flopped down on the hearth rug.

Mrs. Westby was right. He was like a very old dog.

"Do you think he'll always be like this?" she asked.

I shrugged. "We can only hope."

But as I got into my car and drove away I really didn't have much hope. I had seen calves with lung damage after bad pneumonias. They recovered but were called "bad doers" because they remained thin and listless for the rest of their lives. Doctors, too, had plenty of "chesty" people on their books; they were, more or less, in the same predicament.

Weeks and then months went by and the only time I saw the Labrador was when Mrs Westby was walking him on his lead. I always had the impression that he was reluctant to move and his mistress had to stroll along very slowly so that he could keep up with her. The sight of him saddened me when I thought of the lolloping Brandy of old, but I told myself that at least I had saved his life. I could do no more for him now and I made a determined effort to push him out of my mind.

In fact I tried to forget Brandy and managed to do so fairly well until one afternoon in February. On the previous night I felt I had been through the fire. I had treated a colicky horse until 4 a.m. and was crawling into bed, comforted by the knowledge that the animal was settled down and free from pain when I was called to a calving. I had managed to produce a large live calf from a small heifer, but the effort had drained the last of my strength and when I got home it was too late to return to bed.

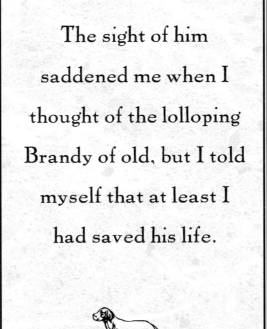

The sight of him saddened me when I thought of the lolloping Brandy of old, but I told myself that at least I had saved his life.

Ploughing through the morning round I was so tired that I felt disembodied, and at lunch Helen watched me anxiously as my head nodded over my food. There were a few dogs in the waiting-room at two o'clock and I dealt with them mechanically, peering through half-closed eyelids. By the time I reached my last patient I was almost asleep on my feet. In fact I had the feeling that I wasn't there at all.

"Next, please," I mumbled as I pushed open the waiting-room door and stood back waiting for the usual sight of a dog being led out to the passage.

But this time there was a big difference. There was a man in the doorway all right and he had a little poodle with him, but the thing that made my eyes snap wide open was that the dog was walking upright on his hind limbs.

I knew I was half-asleep but surely I wasn't seeing things. I stared down at the dog, but the picture hadn't changed—the little creature strutted through the doorway, chest out, head up, as erect as a soldier.

"Follow me, please," I said hoarsely and set off over the tiles to the consulting-room. Halfway along I just had to turn round to check the evidence of my eyes and it was just the same—the poodle, still on his hind legs, marching along unconcernedly at his master's side.

The man must have seen the bewilderment in my face because he burst suddenly into a roar of laughter.

"Don't worry, Mr. Herriot," he said, "this little dog was circus trained before I got him as a pet. I like to show off his little tricks. This one really startles people."

"You can say that again," I said breathlessly. "It nearly gave me heart failure."

The poodle wasn't ill, he just wanted his nails clipping. I smiled as I hoisted him on to the table and began to ply the clippers.

"I suppose he won't want his hind claws doing," I said. "He'll have worn them down himself." I was glad to find I had recovered sufficiently to attempt a little joke.

However, by the time I had finished, the old lassitude had taken over again and I felt ready to fall down as I showed man and dog to the front door.

I watched the little animal trotting away down the street—in the orthodox manner this time—and it came to me suddenly that it had been a long time since I had seen a dog doing something unusual and amusing. Like the things Brandy used to do.

A wave of gentle memories flowed through me as I leaned wearily against the door post and closed my eyes. When I opened them I saw Brandy coming round the corner of the street with Mrs. Westby. His nose was entirely obscured by a large red tomato-soup can and he strained madly at the leash and whipped his tail when he saw me.

It was certainly a hallucination this time. I was looking into the past. I really ought to go to bed immediately. But I was still rooted to the door post when the Labrador bounded up the steps, made an attempt, aborted by the soup can, to lick my face and contented himself with cocking a convivial leg against the bottom step.

I stared into Mrs. Westby's radiant face. "What . . . what . . .?"

With her sparkling eyes and wide smile she looked more attractive than ever. "Look, Mr. Herriot, look! He's better, he's better!"

In an instant I was wide awake. "And I . . . I suppose you'll want me to get that can off him?"

"Oh yes, yes, please!"

It took all my strength to lift him on to the table. He was heavier now than before his illness. I reached for the familiar forceps and began to turn the jagged edges of the can outwards from the nose and mouth. Tomato soup must have been one of his favourites because he was really deeply embedded and it took some time before I was able to slide the can from his face.

I fought off his slobbering attack. "He's back in the dustbins, I see."

"Yes, he is, quite regularly. I've pulled several cans off him myself. And he goes sliding with the children, too." She smiled happily.

Thoughtfully I took my stethoscope from the pocket of my white coat and listened to his lungs. They were wonderfully clear. A slight roughness here and there, but the old cacophony had gone.

I leaned on the table and looked at the great dog with a mixture of thankfulness and incredulity. He was as before, boisterous and full of the joy of living. His tongue lolled in a happy grin and the sun glinted through the surgery window on his sleek golden coat.

"But Mr Herriot," Mrs Westby's eyes were wide, "how on earth has this happened? How has he got better?"

"*Vis medicatrix naturae,*" I replied in tones of deep respect.

"I beg your pardon?"

"The healing power of nature. Something no veterinary surgeon can compete with when it decides to act."

"I see. And you can never tell when this is going to happen?"

"No."

For a few seconds we were silent as we stroked the dog's head, ears and flanks.

"Oh, by the way," I said, "has he shown any renewed interest in the blue jeans?"

"Oh my word, yes! They're in the washing-machine at this very moment. Absolutely covered in mud. Isn't it marvellous!"

Dogs like Brandy have always lightened my life. The ones who do funny things and make me laugh. He was a natural comedian and even his troubles with dustbins had their funny side, but his pneumonia did wipe the smile off my face for quite a long time. It is good to end my book with a story about a genuine doggy character like Brandy, and a story, too, with a happy ending. To this day I really don't know why he got better, but it doesn't matter.

Reprinted from

JAMES HERRIOT'S DOG STORIES ~ 1986

Shotgun

By Stanley Coren

An older dog is still that same puppy that you reared. It still cares; it just lacks stamina and is showing some signs of wear. To illustrate this, let me tell you the story of Shotgun.

Shotgun was a big chocolate-colored Labrador retriever. His owner, Fred, had always liked hunting water birds when he lived on the east coast. When he moved to the beautiful countryside of British Columbia, in Western Canada, the plan of owning a gun dog and returning to hunting as a fall pastime seemed ideal. It never quite worked out that way. When Shotgun was only seven months old, Fred's job took him back to the city. Shortly thereafter, Fred married, and when Shotgun was around two, Fred and his wife Clara had their

"At Day's End" ~ John Silver

"The old dog barks backward without getting up.

I can remember when he was a pup."

—ROBERT FROST

first child, Melissa. Somehow, training the dog for hunting just never worked out. Shotgun became a city dog and a family dog. He learned the routines of city life and over a period of six years watched the family grow with the addition of two boys, Steven and Daniel. While Shotgun had never been trained to hunt, he had gone through a beginners dog obedience course taught in a local church and knew all the basic commands. His job was mainly to be a plaything for the children, a companion for Fred and Clara, and the ever-vigilant watchdog who sounded the alarm at the occurrence of any new or suspicious sound or unusual condition around the house.

Time passed, and Shotgun was now eleven years of age, which is old for a Labrador retriever. He moved more slowly and had given up trying to jump on the sofa. He seemed content to sleep more hours than before, although he could still be stirred for short romps with the children, whom he seemed to view as his particular charges. He ran more slowly, though, and no longer jumped very high when chasing a ball or Frisbee, and he tired a bit more easily. His hearing was going, and he responded more slowly and a bit less reliably to the commands that he had learned so many years before. But many things were still the same. He knew when it was time for a walk and

stationed himself expectantly at the door each afternoon from around three o'clock on, waiting for the children's return from school. He continued to sleep nights in the middle of the living room floor, and, as he had always done, he would patrol the house every hour or so, sticking his nose into each of the children's bedrooms and then checking on Fred and Clara before returning to his central post in the living room.

One summer night, Shotgun arose with the feeling that something was definitely wrong. There was smoke in the house, and if the windows and inner doors had not been open, the whole place would already have been filled with the noxious fumes of burning materials. The dog began to bark furiously to rouse the household, but nothing happened. Moving as quickly as his arthritic body would allow, he entered Fred and Clara's room. His barking still did not cause them to rise, so with a great deal of effort the dog painfully leapt up on the bed, placing his front paws on Fred's chest and barking loudly. Fred sputtered to a confused state of wakefulness. He immediately became aware of the smoke and wakened Clara. Fred and Clara rushed to the rooms of the two young boys, each grabbing one of them, and raced through the now flame-filled house toward the outside. Both shouted for Melissa, the oldest at nine, assuming that

> One summer night, Shotgun arose with the feeling that something was definitely wrong.

Daniel-

the noise and commotion would get her up and moving from her bedroom in the rear of the house. When the two of them reached the front lawn and looked back, most of the house was covered with flames. Fire trucks were arriving, but Melissa was nowhere in sight. Fred tried to dash back into the house, but the heat and the flames were too much for his bare feet, and he was forced to retreat.

Shotgun was still inside. Perhaps somewhere in that great old head of his, he had remembered to count and knew that one of his charges was missing. He slowly lumbered into Melissa's room, only to find her standing

"Fidelity" ~ Nigel Hemming

in the midst of the smoke, bewildered and crying. Shotgun barked and moved toward the door, but Melissa didn't understand or was too confused to follow. He then gently grabbed the ruffled sleeve of her nightgown and began to pull her toward the door. The front of the house was completely impassable, so the old dog turned, half dragging and half guiding the frightened girl toward the rear entrance. As the flames leapt around them, they were confronted with the rear screen door, which had been secured with a simple hook and eye latch. Perhaps, had he been younger and more agile, Shotgun could have pushed through the screen mesh, but at that moment it seemed to be an impenetrable barrier. Melissa was too stunned to help and stood in a daze. Shotgun dropped her sleeve for a moment and reared up on his hind legs. He then pushed up on the screen door latch to unhook it, a technique that had brought him a severe reprimand several years before when, as a younger dog, he had used it to open the back door in order to respond to the harassment of a fox terrier that had learned how to enter the backyard and had a fondness for digging in the small vegetable garden.

Shotgun's manipulations were not as deft as they used to be, and as he pushed his nose against the hook, it tore his skin. Still, he persisted, and the latch rose from its eyelet, and the door flew open. Shotgun again grabbed Melissa's sleeve and pulled her to the center of the yard before letting her go and turning to the task of licking at his singed paws. Moments later, the fire fighters arrived to find Melissa with her arms around Shotgun's neck, sobbing quietly, and stroking his bleeding muzzle where the screen door hook had cut him.

Shotgun was old, slow, and less reliable than he had been in years past. Yet he was still the self-appointed protector of the house, and his intelligence and problem-solving ability were completely dedicated to his masters' safety and well-being. Old certainly does not mean dumb, useless, or spent. Shotgun had shown great intelligence that night. He had figured out that something was wrong, then had solved the problem of waking his sleeping masters to warn them. He had discerned that one child was missing and had found the answer to the dilemma of how to bring her through the house. When faced with the predicament of the front door blocked by fire, he had found an alternative solution, and when confronted with the latched back door, he had solved the last problem standing in the way of their escape. The five human beings who made up his pack, his family, his masters, all owed their lives to that old brain's information processing and problem solving.

Reprinted from

THE INTELLIGENCE OF DOGS ~ 1994

"Puppy Love" ~ Kevin Daniel

It's a Dog's Life

By Gene Hill

No matter how much you paid for that doggie in the window, it's nothing compared to the cost of keeping him.

I recently found a newspaper clipping that claimed to estimate what it costs to own a dog. Based on a life expectancy of eleven years, the total came to about $13,000—not counting the cost of the dog. The expenses broke down as follows: food, $4,500; vet bills, $3,300; training, $2,000; grooming supplies, $1,200; collars, toys, and leashes, another $1,200; and flea and bug stuff, $900.

I suppose that's accurate for an average non-sporting dog. But as the owner of various hunting dogs, I'd like to offer an additional list of items you could call "miscellaneous." If you're a gun dog owner, your

"The Book Lover" ~ John Silver

"Never judge a dog's pedigree

by the kind of books he does not chew."

—Anonymous

list might deviate somewhat, but probably not by much. I'll leave it to you to fill in the costs.

Lab puppy: free, given to me by a friend who bought it at a DU dinner and, on sober reflection, decided against adding it to his household. New station wagon to transport dog, and kennel for same. House kennel (still unused), dog dish, dog bed. Training dummies, whistles, dummy launcher, blank cartridge pistol with holster. Hip boots, waders. New farm complete with pond. Boat for pond. Books on Lab training. Books telling what wonderful dogs Labs are. Lab prints, glasses with Labs on them. Lab doormat in case strangers didn't hear the racket that ensued at the ring of the doorbell. Field trial clubs with accompanying dues. New 12-gauge to serve as trial gun. New 12-gauge for duck shooting. New wardrobe for field trials and duck hunts.

After the dog is six months old, growth requires these items: new leashes, collars, and dummies. Sessions with professional trainer; travel to other trial grounds for participation and observation. Neckties with Labs on them. Upholstery repair for station wagon. Dog bed for wagon. New 20-gauge for upland gunning with Lab; new wardrobe for same.

At a year or year and a half, the expenses seem to level off. Normal wear and tear necessitates replacing some items, but these expenses are nothing you can't handle by making such simple sacrifices as cutting out restaurants, forgoing name-brand beverages at home, and discovering tasty tuna helpers and meat substitutes.

At this point many Lab owners, myself included, suffer a form of amnesia or mental derangement known medically as *multi-canis*, the seriousness of which varies. The addition of one Lab is the most common result, but acquisitions of two or three are commonly observed. Curiously, the victim seems content, and may appear normal to all but the immediate family. Second mortgages are not uncommon at this stage.

Perversely, the worst thing that can happen to a Lab owner is that one or more of the dogs shows field trial promise. If this happens, large four-wheel-drive vehicles and dog trailers are thrown into the balance. Phone bills for calls to famous trainers resemble the annual budget of the welfare program the afflicted dog owner seems destined for. Maps with directions to remote and desolate swamps decorate the kitchen table where nourishing food was once served. Birthday and anniversary dates are replaced in the memory by pedigrees and blood-line characteristics; the vet doubles as the family doctor.

Then you must consider the following: upholstered chairs gutted because of curiosity or dissatisfaction; expensive shrubs and flowers excavated for the same reason. Rugs, blankets, pillows, chairs, boots, shoes, decoys, lamp cords, gloves, and books used for teething. Gifts to frightened delivery persons. New door screening and paint. Replacing wallpaper soaked by flying spray from wet coats. Glassware and china swept off tables by wagging tails. Removal of dog hair from moving parts of washer, drier, and refrigerator. Gifts to cat-owning neighbor.

To be honest, I'd guess that my Labs cost almost as much per year to raise and keep as a child, but this is hard to quantify. Both exhibit roughly the same table manners, but one marks doubles better than the other. Labs are easier to housebreak, but children can learn to do helpful chores. Generally, it's a wash.

I'm not going to discuss pointing dogs, since my experience with them is limited, but it would be foolish to think that, as with the Labs, anything less than a third of your annual income (net) could suffice. If you think I jest, remember that a lot of pointing dog country is in the South, where it's practically law that if you have a couple of high-stepping pointers, you need a high-stepping horse to complete the picture—or at least a high-stepping four-wheel-drive.

Finally, I'm sure you have often heard the old expression "going to the dogs." Remember the picture it conjures? Some poor soul in tatters and bent by care . . . not an inaccurate portrait of myself, your faithful scrivener, toiling by guttering candlelight for the means to purchase a few bones, and hoping that when the dogs are through, there'll be something left for my soup.

Reprinted from

FIELD & STREAM ~ 1993

"If you pick up a starving dog and make him prosperous, he will not bite you.

"Farm Life" ~ Nigel Hemming

This is the principal difference between a dog and a man." —MARK TWAIN

Dove Tactics
for the Ethically Bankrupt and the Morally Depraved

By O. Victor Miller, Jr.

"And oft I heard the tender dove
In firry woodlands making moan."

—TENNYSON

"That's a pretty good retriever you've got there," says Mark Slappey, a fellow guest on a dove shoot near Cobb, Georgia. "She's picked up six of my birds and five of Lee's."

"Well, let me give you a couple of doves then," I say. "I about got my mess."

Looks like I'm high man on the field again, without firing a shot, on a pay hunt George McIntosh and his son Jarrett invited me on

"Waiting to Pounce" ~ Nigel Hemming

because I lied, telling them I was an outdoor sportswriter for a popular magazine.

"That's the busiest dog I believe I ever saw," says George, lumping his cheek with his tongue. "How many birds you got?"

"Oh, I don't know. Close to a dozen." Actually, I know exactly how many doves are in my game bag. I've learned to count carefully, since game warden Jeff Swift gave me a ticket last year for having thirteen, one bird over the bag limit. Swift said he believed me when I told him I hadn't killed any of the birds, that my dog retrieved other peoples', miscounting in her enthusiasm the supernumerary dove. As a matter of fact, I confessed, I'd gone into the field without any shotgun shells, having forgotten to buy any.

Jeff said: "I'm not giving you this ticket for killing thirteen birds. I'm giving it to you for having thirteen birds in your possession.

In court Judge John Salter said he believed me too, but that he was going to fine me as an incentive to teach Geechee, my chocolate Lab, to count better. "For the time being," he said, gathering his brow and hammering his gavel, "at least until Geechee gets more mathematically precise, I want you to get down there and *help* your dog count birds."

Training Geechee to retrieve other peoples' downed quarry occurred quite naturally, resulting from an accidental combination of my Lab's blooded hyperactivity and my poor marksmanship. When she was a pup, she dutifully sat by my side while I blasted holes in the troposphere. Finally disgusted, she began snapping at my legs and barking, compounding my ballistic inaccuracy. It's hard enough to lead and follow through a moving target without having to worry about tooth-tracks in your ankles and ass, which is how I happened upon my dove tactics. As soon as I discovered Geechee's willingness to retrieve other hunters' birds, I trained her to ignore my whistle and my arm-flapping as I ostensibly called her back. It's easier than you think to train your dog to pay absolutely no attention to command.

In the old days, my shell per bird ratio sounded like women's church league batting

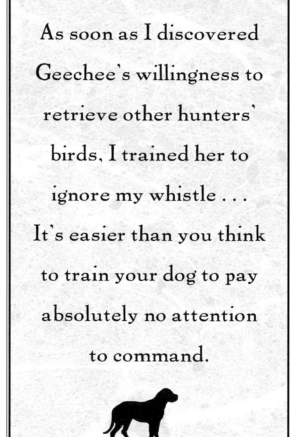

> As soon as I discovered Geechee's willingness to retrieve other hunters' birds, I trained her to ignore my whistle . . . It's easier than you think to train your dog to pay absolutely no attention to command.

averages, but I changed all that, and since I've retired from dove hunting altogether, I'm willing to pass on a few machiavellian secrets. Since training my Lab to go after every bird on the field, and observing a few common sense hunting tactics, I increased my bird to shot ratio dramatically. Often I bagged three or more birds per shot, and I didn't have to resort to shooting them from power lines either or waiting for them to puddle up on the ground. Most days I got my limit without popping a cap.

Having a dog gave me a visible excuse for encroaching on the best stand on the field. Geechee could usually get to my neighbors' downed bird before my neighbor could. This gave me reason to invade his territory—I'm returning his bird. "That damn dog," I'd say. Sometimes I'd even pluck the bird for him.

If my neighbor's birds didn't fall in range of my retriever, I could still usurp his position under the guise of searching out a cripple. Before approaching a fellow hunter, I'd unload my shotgun and reload with empty casings, for safety sake and for reasons I'll soon divulge.

"Dead bird! Dead bird!" I call as I wander into a fellow hunter's field of fire, making elaborate hand signals. I politely offer to hunt any of his lost birds while I'm finding mine. There is always, by the way, a snaky area near a good dove stand because poisonous reptiles know the best places to gather for heavenly windfalls, but Geechee is immune to hemotoxin, having been snakebit on numerous occasions.

At this point I usually give my neighbor one of his own birds, a good investment if his spot is good enough to hang around for a while. I ask him, "You see where my cripple fell, friend?"

"I must've been facing the other way," he'll say.

I hang around and chit-chat until a bird flies over. "Your bird," I'll say, and he'll say, "Naw, go ahead."

We bicker amicably until the bird is directly overhead. Then we both throw up. It's easy to watch your neighbor out the corner of your eye and to synchronize. After he shoots, I eject an empty casing. "Dead bird," I yell to Geechee, who brings me the dove, of course. "Did you shoot too?" I ask my host as he reloads. "How about that! We must've

shot at the exact same time. I didn't hear your gun go off. Gosh, this could be your bird. I'll bet it is!"

"Naw, keep the bird."

If my neighbor downs a double, I'm careful not to claim both birds, but I'll remove two empty shells from my double barrel, protesting that I couldn't have killed both birds, no way.

"Well, if you knock any down you can't find, just holler and I'll come back over."

Sometimes surveillance is necessary, sometimes not.

With my binoculars I carefully tally the number of doves downed by surrounding hunters, noting cripples and lost birds.

If I can find a bird that puts him over the limit, he'll insist I keep it. It's an easy thing for a dove hunter to give up a bird he's already counted lost, especially if the recovered bird mandates that he stop shooting and zip his shotgun case. Another reason I like to see the DNR attending.

Well, you may interject, my problem isn't so much bagging dove as it is getting on a decent hunt to begin with—the ones with barbecue, pretty girls, and flocks that darken the sky.

So sometimes I just ride around the countryside until I happen upon a hunt that looks good enough to crash. I like to see a DNR truck in attendance, indicating that the field isn't baited. Also dove hunters are less likely to shoot you and your retriever if the law is there. Using my methods, I could fill my limit quickly and quit the field before potentially embarrassing post hunt socializing begins, but sometimes I stay for the barbecue, where I try to charm my way into next Saturday's hunt.

My tactics work best with people who don't know me, so lunchtime Saturday on opening day of dove season found me cruizing around in my pick-up looking for a gathering of dove shooters preparing to convoy to the country. I walked around introducing myself and offering soft drinks until I found out who the host was, gleaning simultaneously a half dozen names I could drop in order to establish legitimacy. When I identify a host, I sometimes thank him for allowing Sam or Bill or whoever I've just met for letting me tag along, but more often than not I just join the procession. The cooler of iced down drinks also allowed me to orbit the field offering refreshments while casing the best stands. The cost of the drinks was nominal when you consider I no longer bought shotgun shells.

If anybody called me on the legitimacy of my attendance, I slapped my forehead, claiming I'd joined the wrong hunt. "Damn my thick skull," I'd say, "you mean this ain't Bubba an' 'em's hunt?" If caught irrefutably red-handed, I'd wait for the December season and claim I'd been born again, worthy

> If anybody called me on the legitimacy of my attendance, I slapped my forehead, claiming I'd joined the wrong hunt. . . "you mean this ain't Bubba an' 'ems's hunt?"

once more of restoration into the society of men.

Thus, it follows that another way to establish legitimacy among strangers is to say you're new in the area and the preacher invited you. There's always a preacher with a different notion of fellowship than cliquish dove hunters have. Nobody's likely to raise an eyebrow against a preacher using a dove shoot to recruit the fallen.

"Preacher? What Preacher?" an unpolished countryman once challenged.

"The Baptist preacher, of course," I reply, figuring that's as safe a bet as there is in Dixie.

"What?" snarls the roughneck, who turns out to be the Methodist clergyman. "He here too?"

But one Sunday morning a fateful misadventure occurred that made me stop dove hunting altogether. Which is why I'm willing to publish my tactics.

I should've sensed trouble when I saw the hunters wore Nikes instead of snake boots and had removed their dogs' collars. The hunters looked a little rough but, what the hell, the hunting brotherhood is a democratic tribe, transcending socio-economic stratification. There were plenty of doves feeding in the field, I'd verified by a phone call the night before to a good old boy who could see the field from the deck of his doublewide, "They's so many doves on the power lines it's dimming the lights." Sure enough, when I got there before daylight guns were already blasting away.

In the first light I see vortexes reel flurry like dustdevils. Boy oh boy. The doves swarm the field angrily, falling like feathered manna beneath the blazing gunfire, which sounds like a brushfire in a stand of bamboo.

Geechee vibrates with anticipation. I unleash her and she bounces around like a jackrabbit, amassing birds quickly. Then I see a glint of a patent leather holster belt and a speeding four-wheeler trailing a plume of dark dust against the crimson sky.

Hunters quit the field, vanishing into peripheral fringe and planted pines. It's as though Corporal Swift speeds toward the central pivot of a spinning turntable that centrifugally slings hunters off the field.

He skids to a stop, obscured for a moment in his own dust. "You!" he says, dismounting and producing a pad from his hip pocket.

"Hey, I wasn't shooting. Why, I didn't even bring any shotgun shells. My shotgun's plugged and I'm two birds under the limit."

"This ticket's for hunting over bait."

"Bait?"

"How d'you think these peanut hearts got in this corn field?"

I glance between my feet. The ground is covered with a variety of extraneous silage, including a fodder that looks like granola party mix.

Meanwhile Geechee realizes the windfall of an abandoned field. She begins sniffing out discarded evidence, trotting it over, dropping birds at our feet and wagging her stubby tail.

"Stay, Geechee!" I command. "Sit!"

Geechee trots off again, obediently ignorant, panting happily and winking over her shoulder.

"Those aren't my birds," I insist.

"That's your Lab, ain't it? The same one you told Judge Salter you'd teach arithmetic. And it looks like these birds are in your possession since you're the only one hunting."

Geechee trots up, grinning around the fluttering bird in her mouth. "That makes fifteen, don't it?" says Swift.

"Look Jeff, I didn't know this field was baited. I don't even know whose land this is." I run Geechee down and snap a leash on her collar. She bares her canines and growls like an idling weed-whacker. It's hard to restrain a conscientious dog once she gets started, but I finally collar her and bring her back to the four-wheeler, tangling up in a tumbleweed of peanut vines.

Officer Swift lifts his black cap with his thumb and index finger, scratching his bald spot with his pinkie. He watches the sky for an angel or a UFO. Then he licks the point of his pencil. "You say you're trespassing too?"

Reprinted with permission from the author

50

"In the Doghouse" ~ Nigel Hemming

"The great pleasure of a dog is that you make a fool of yourself with him and not only will he not scold you, but he will make a fool of himself, too."

—SAMUEL BUTLER

Ike,
A Good Friend

By Gary Paulsen

Much of my childhood I was alone. Family troubles—my parents were drunks—combined with a devastating shyness and a complete lack of social skills to ensure a life of solitude. This isolation was not natural, of course, especially for a child, and most of the time I was excruciatingly lonely. I sought friends whenever I could, but was rarely successful.

When I was very young these times of aloneness were spent making model airplanes, reading comic books or just daydreaming. But when I was twelve, living in a small town named Twin Forks in northern Minnesota, an uncle gave me a Remington .22 rifle he'd bought at a hardware store for ten dollars. I ran to the woods.

"Portrait of Two Black Labs" ~ Nigel Hemming

"All knowledge, the totality of all questions and answers,

is contained in the dog."

—FRANZ KAFKA

It is not somehow "politically correct" to hunt, and that is a shame for young boys. For me it was not only the opening into a world of wonder, it was salvation. I lived and breathed to hunt, to fish.

Two rivers ran out of town, one to the north and one to the east, and any day, hour or few minutes I could spare I would run these rivers. The first year I hunted mostly rabbits and ruffed grouse—feeding myself in the process. I scuffled along in old boots with a box of .22 long rifle cartridges in my pocket and the single-shot rifle in my hand. On my back was an old army surplus light pack I'd bought with money from setting pins at the local bowling alley. In the pack I had matches, usually a loaf of bread, salt and an old aluminum pot for boiling water.

There was great beauty in running the rivers, especially in the fall when the leaves were turning. The maples were red gold and filtered the sunlight so that you could almost taste the richness of the light, and before long I added a surplus army blanket, rolled up over the pack, and I would spend the nights out as well.

During school—where I did badly—I would hunt in the evenings. But on Friday I was gone, and I would frequently spend the entire weekend alone in the woods.

The problem was that I was alone. I had not learned then to love solitude—as I do now—and the feeling of loneliness was visceral, palpable. I would see something beautiful—the sun through the leaves, a deer moving through the dappled light, the explosion of a grouse flying up through the leaves—and I would turn to point it out to somebody, turn to say, "Look. . ." and there would be no one there.

The second fall after I'd started living in and off the woods I decided to hunt ducks. Miles to the north were the great swamps and breeding grounds of literally millions of ducks and geese, and when the migratory flights started south the sky would seem to darken with them. The .22 rifle was not suited for ducks—was indeed illegal for them—so I saved my money setting pins and bought an old single-shot Browning twelve-gauge shotgun from a kid named Sonny. The gun had a long barrel and a full choke, and with number four shot seemed to reach out forever. I never became really good with it, but could hit now and then when the ducks were flying at the right angle. Duck hunting soon became my life.

I did not have decoys but I made some blinds six miles out of town where there were cattail swamps. I would walk out there in the dark, leaving the house at three in the morning, nestle into the blinds and wait for the morning flights to come in from the north. Usually I would get one or two ducks—once a goose—but some I wounded or didn't kill cleanly and they would get into the swamp grass and weeds in the water and I couldn't find them.

It was about then that I met Ike.

Ike was a great barrel-chested black Labrador that became one of the best friends I've ever had and was in all ways an equal; not a pet, not something to master, but an equal.

I had had other dogs. Snowball in the Philippines, then a cocker spaniel somebody gave me named Trina. They were sweet and dear and gave love the way only dogs can, with total acceptance, but Ike was the first dog I'd ever known not as a pet but as a separate entity, a partner.

We met strangely enough. It was duck season and I was going hunting. I woke up at three and sneaked from the basement, where I stayed when my parents were drunk—

which was all the time—up into the kitchen. Quietly I made two fried egg sandwiches at the stove. I wrapped them in cellophane (this was well before sandwich bags), folded them into a paper sack and put them in my pack along with a Thermos of hot coffee. Then I got my shotgun from the basement. I dumped a box of shells into the pockets of the old canvas coat I'd found in a trunk in the back of the coal room. I put on the knee-high rubber boots I'd bought at army surplus.

I walked from the apartment building four blocks to the railroad, crossed the tracks near the roundhouse yard, crossed the Eighth Street bridge and then dropped down to the riverbank and started walking along the water.

The river quickly left settled country and headed into woods, and in the dark—there was just the faintest touch of gray on the horizon—it was hard going. The brush pulled at my clothes and after a mile and a half the swamps became more prevalent so that I was wading in muck. I went to pull myself up the bank and walk where the ground was harder.

It had been raining, mixed with snow, and the mud on the bank was as slick as grease. I fell once in the darkness, got to my feet and scrabbled up the bank again, shotgun in one hand and grabbing at roots and shrubs with the other. I had just gained the top, brought my head up over the edge, when a part of the darkness detached itself, leaned close to my face and went:

"Woof."

Nigel Hemming

"A Wintery Day" ~ Nigel Hemming

It was that distinct—not "arf," nor "ruff," nor a growl, but the very defined sound of "woof."

I was so startled that I froze, mouth half open. Then I let go of the shrub and fell back down the mud incline. On the way down the thought hit me—bear. Something big and black, that sound—it had to be a bear. Then the word *gun*. I had a gun. I landed on my back and aimed up the bank, pulled the hammer back and put my finger on the trigger before I realized the gun wasn't loaded yet. I never loaded it while walking in the dark. I clawed at my pockets for shells, found one, broke open the gun and inserted a shell, slammed it shut and was going to aim again when something about the shape stopped me. (It was well it did—I had accidentally jammed the barrel of the shotgun full of mud when I fell. Had I pulled the trigger the shell would have blown up in my face.)

There was just enough of the dawn to show a silhouette. Whatever it was remained at the top of the bank. It was sitting there looking down at me and was the wrong shape and size for a bear. It was a big dog, a black dog. But it was a dog and it wasn't attacking.

I lowered the gun and wiped the mud out of my eyes, stood and scraped mud off my clothes. I was furious, but not at the dog. There were other hunters who worked the river during duck season and some of them had dogs. I assumed that one of them was nearby and had let his animal run loose, scaring about ten years off my life.

"Who owns you?" I asked the shape. It didn't move or make any further sounds and I climbed the bank again and it moved back a few feet, then sat again.

"Hello!" I called into the woods around me. "I have your dog here!"

There was nobody.

"So you're a stray?" There were many stray dogs in town and some of them ran to the woods. It was bad when they did because they often formed packs and did terrible damage. In packs they were worse than wolves because they did not fear men the way wolves did and they tore livestock and some people to pieces.

But strays were shy and usually starved. This dog stayed near me and in the gathering light I could see that he was a Labrador and that he was well fed. His coat was thick and he had fat on his back and sides.

"Well," I said. "What do I do with you?"

This time his tail thumped twice and he pointedly looked at the gun, then back at my face, then down the side of the river to the water.

"You want to hunt?"

There, he knew that word. His tail hammered his sides and he stood, wiggling, and moved off along the river ahead of me.

I had never hunted with a dog before and did not know for certain what was expected of me. But I started to follow, thinking we might jump up a mallard or teal. Then I remembered my fall and the mud and that the gun was still loaded. I unloaded it and checked the bore and found the end packed with mud. It took me a minute to clean it out and reload it and before I'd finished he'd come back and sat four feet away, watching me quietly.

It was light enough now for me to see that he had a collar and a tag so he wasn't a stray. It must be some town dog, I thought, that had followed me. I held out my hand. "Come here . . ."

But he remained at a distance and when it was obvious that I was ready to go he set off again. It was light enough now to shoot— light enough to see the front bead of the shotgun and a duck against the sky—so I kept the gun ready and we had not gone fifty yards when two mallards exploded out of some thick grass near the bank about twenty yards away and started up and across the river.

It was a classic shot. Mallards flying straight up to gain altitude before making off, backlit against a cold, cloudy October sky. I raised the gun, cocked it, aimed just above the right-hand duck to lead his flight and squeezed the trigger.

There was a crash and the recoil slammed me back. I was small and the gun was big and I usually had a bruise after firing it more than once. But my aim was good and the right-hand duck seemed to break in the air, crumpled and fell into the water. I had shot ducks over the river before and the way to get them was to wait until the current brought the body to shore. Sometimes it took most of the morning, waiting for the slow-moving water to bring them in.

This time was different. With the smell of powder still in the air, almost before the duck finished falling, the dog was off the bank in a great leap, hit the water swimming, his shoulders pumping as he churned the surface and made a straight line to the dead duck. He took it in his mouth gently, turned and swam back, climbed the bank and put the duck by my right foot, then moved off a couple of feet and sat, looking at me.

I made sure the duck was dead, then picked it up and tied it to my belt with a string I carried for the purpose. The dog sat and watched me the whole time, waiting. It was fully light now and I moved to him, petted him—he let me but in a reserved way—and pulled his tag to the side so I could read it.

My name is Ike.

That's all it said. No address, no owner's name, just one short sentence.

"Well, Ike"—at this his tail wagged—"I'd like to thank you for bringing me the duck . . ."

And that was how it started, how I came to know Ike.

Duck season soon consumed me and I spent every morning walking and hunting the river. On school days I would go out and come back just in time to get to classes and on the weekends I stayed out.

And every morning Ike was there. I'd come across the bridge, start down the river, and he'd be there, waiting. After a few mornings he'd let me pet him—I think he did it for me more than him—and by the end of the first week I was looking forward to seeing him. By the middle of the second week I felt as if we'd been hunting with each other forever.

And he knew hunting. Clearly somebody had trained him well. He moved quietly, sat in the blind with me without moving, watched the barrel of the gun to see which duck I was going to shoot at, and when I shot he would leap into the water. On those occasions when I missed—I think more often than not—he would watch the duck fly away, turn to me and give me a look of such uncompromising pity and scorn that I would feel compelled to apologize and make excuses.

"The wind moved the barrel," or "A drop of water hit my eye when I shot."

Of course, he did not believe me but would turn back, sitting there waiting for the next shot so I could absolve myself.

When the hunting was done he'd walk back with me to town, trotting alongside, until we arrived at the bridge. There he would stop and sit down and nothing I did would make him come farther. I tried waiting him out to see where he would go but when it was obvious that I wasn't going to leave he merely lay down and went to sleep, or turned and started back into the woods, looking back to see if we were going hunting again.

Once I left him, crossed the bridge and then hid in back of a building and watched. He stayed until I was out of sight and then turned and trotted north away from the bridge along the river. There were no houses in that direction, at least on the far side of the river, and I watched him until he disappeared into the woods. I was no wiser than I had been.

The rest of his life was a mystery and would remain so for thirty years. But when we were together we became fast friends, at least on my part.

I would cook an extra egg sandwich for Ike and when the flights weren't coming we would "talk." That is to say, I would talk, tell him all my troubles, and he would sit, his enormous head sometimes resting on my knee, his huge brown eyes looking up at me while I petted him and rattled on.

On the weekends when I stayed out, I would construct a lean-to and make a fire, and he would curl up on the edge of my blanket. Many mornings I would awaken to find him under the frost-covered blanket with me, sound asleep, my arm thrown over him, his breath rumbling against my side.

It seemed like there'd always been an Ike in my life and then one morning he wasn't there and I never saw him again. I tried to find him. I would wait for him in the morning by the bridge, but he never showed again. I thought he might have gotten hit by a car, or his owners moved away. I mourned him and missed him. But I did not learn what happened to him for thirty years.

I grew and went into the crazy parts of life, army and those other mistakes a young man could make. I grew older and got back into dogs, this time sled dogs, and ran the Iditarod race across Alaska. After my first run I came back to Minnesota with slides of the race to show to all the people who had supported me. A sporting goods store had been one of my sponsors and I gave a public slide show of the race one evening.

There was an older man sitting in a wheelchair and I saw that when I told a story of how Cookie, my lead dog, had saved my life his eyes teared up and he nodded quietly.

When the event was over he wheeled up to me and shook my hands.

"I had a dog like your Cookie—a dog that saved my life."

"Oh—did you run sleds?"

He shook his head. "No. Not like that. I lived up in Twin Forks when I was young and was drafted to serve in the Korean War. I had a Labrador that I raised and hunted with, and left him when I went away. I was gone just under a year; I got wounded and lost the use of my legs. When I came back from the hospital he was waiting there and he spent the rest of his life by my side. I would have gone crazy without him. I'd sit for hours and talk to him and he would listen quietly . . . it was so sad. He loved to hunt and I never hunted again." He faded off and his eyes were moist again. "I still miss him . . ."

I looked at him, then out the window of the sporting goods store. It was spring and the snow was melting outside but I was seeing fall and a boy and a Lab sitting in a duck blind. Twin Forks, he'd said—and the Korean War. The time was right, and the place, and the dog.

"Your dog," I said. "Was he named Ike?"

He smiled and nodded. "Why, yes—but how . . . did you know him?"

There was a soft spring rain starting and the window misted with it. That was why Ike had not come back. He had another job.

"Yes," I said, turning to him. "He was my friend. . . ."

dividers

Reprinted from

MY LIFE IN DOG YEARS ~ 1998

(following spread)
"Higher Ground" ~ Kevin Daniel

KevinDaniel-97

Exit
Laughing

By Ed Zern

The late George Murnane was not only a noted financier but a keen sportsman and a fancier of Labrador retrievers, whose superbly trained dogs won the National Open Retriever Field Trial several times. George lived on Long Island and spent much of his time with people who, like himself, took Labrador retrievers and field trials seriously, and were highly competitive. I called him one time to congratulate him on his having won the Open for the second time, or on one of his Labs having won it, and asked how it felt to be a two-time winner of this prestigious event. He said, "Ed, the most interesting thing about winning the Open is observing the consternation of one's friends."

"On the Lookout" ~ Nigel Hemming

At that time George employed his own full-time trainer, Joe Schomer, and maintained a kennel of about ten Labs, each of which was potentially capable, in the opinion of George and/or Joe, of winning the National Open on a good day. If it became apparent that a promising dog wasn't quite good enough, George gave it to someone who he thought could provide a good home for it and would, he hoped, use it in the field or duck marsh, because he knew the joy that Labs take in retrieving. When a mutual friend recommended me as a suitable donee, George called me one time and said he had a 16-month-old male Lab, sired by FTC Hiwood My Delight, his favorite Lab of all those he had ever owned. He said the pup was a charming character but was too intelligent and independent to make a great field-trial dog, and offered to let me have him. The next Saturday my wife and I drove out to Syosset, saw the young dog, found him instantly irresistible, thanked George and his wife Edith, herself an amateur handler in

field trials, loaded him into the station wagon and drove home.

We had picked up a bench at an antique shop along the way, and while I was getting it out of the wagon the new member of the family (whose kennel name was Wull or Wullie) disappeared. I was concerned, as we lived in a thickly settled suburb in which it's easy for a strange pooch to get confused, and blew loudly on the Thunderer whistle to which Wullie had been trained. When this got no response I was about to take off to search

the area when Evelyn said "Look!" Trotting across the lawn was Wullie, with a magnificent uncooked crown rib roast of lamb, complete with paper pantaloons on the rib ends, held carefully in his mouth. He came up to us with his tail wagging happily, sat proudly in front of me to deliver, as he'd been trained to do, and when I took the roast from him, noting with pleasure that he had a "soft mouth," he beamed with doggy joy and said in Labrador retriever body-language, "I know it's not a duck, boss, but it's the best I could do under the circumstances, and I hope you like it. We're going to make a great team!"

With Wull stashed in the house I took off in the direction he had come from, and when I asked my neighbor George if he was missing a crown roast of lamb, and told him why I asked, he said it wasn't his but not to worry, as I'd surely hear from someone and in no uncertain terms. I scoured the neighborhood, knocking on doors both front and back, trying to find a distraught housewife or cook bereft of dinner with six guests due to arrive shortly, but had no success. When I got back to the house, we telephoned every meat market and butcher in the area, trying to learn who had delivered a world-class crown roast of lamb to someone in the neighborhood that afternoon and had no doubt left it on the back porch. That was twenty-odd years ago, and to this day I haven't had a clue; once or twice a month since then I take a brief break in whatever I'm doing and try to figure where Wullie found that roast.

Being around Wull always put me in mind of the story about the man who dropped in to see a friend and found him playing chess with a poodle. When he expressed surprise, the friend said, "It's no big deal. I beat him most of the time." I'm fairly sure I could have taught Wullie to play a fair game, although he might have had trouble, as do I, with some of the currently fashionable Queen's Bishop Pawn openings, and I'd have had him concentrate on Ruy Lopez and other conservative maneuvers. He was bored to tears by training dummies, and barely tolerated the shackled ducks used at minor field trials. On occasion he would mark and find a shackled duck, pick it up and contemptuously flip it high in the air, which didn't endear him to field-trial judges, who are inclined to be stuffy. But in a duck blind he was sensational, spotting approaching birds far across the marsh long before I saw them, and having an uncanny ability to know that a duck had been pinked by one or two stray pellets even when I was sure I had missed clean; he would take off hell-for-leather across the marsh in pursuit and almost always come back after 10 or 15 minutes with a fairly healthy bird in his soft mouth. Sometimes the bird I had missed (?) was a black duck and he returned with a broadbill; but I figured that was a matter between Wull and his conscience, and didn't complain. He had a choke-bored nose and hunted grouse and woodcock with immense pleasure, but never learned to hold a point more than a few seconds. That retriever knew I wanted him to hold point, but figured the hell with it.

Wull died at a ripe old age, but some of his genes are present in one or two of Gene Hill's Labs who are his great-great-great granddaughters. He was the only

> He was bored to tears by training dummies . . . But in a duck blind he was sensational.

animal I've ever owned, except for a Capuchin monkey now in its 18th year, that had extrasensory perception, and I'd cite a few examples except that you wouldn't believe them. One time, spending a weekend with Wullie at Sam Eskin's country house in Woodstock I told Sam that Wull was the only dog I'd ever known that had intellectual curiosity, and understandably Sam accused me of galloping anthropomorphism. I didn't argue the point, but was gratified next day when Sam called me to the window and pointed to a wading pool in the garden with lily pads floating on the surface. Wullie was standing in 6 inches of water, very carefully turning over leaf after leaf with his right paw and peering at the undersides, which were crawling with small snails. It was the first time I had realized he was interested in gastropody, but it didn't surprise me.

At that time I drove an Austin-Healy roadster, usually faster than was absolutely necessary, and Wullie loved riding in the passenger seat, especially with the top down. The other two Labs rode on the floor under the dashboard, but Wull liked to see where he was going, and enjoyed scenery. He quickly learned to lean into curves as we came into them, and wasn't happy unless we were going really fast. One time with the top down I passed a highway-patrol car going the opposite direction on the Taconic Parkway, and figuring the fuzz would estimate my speed and come after me I pulled off onto the shoulder and waited. Sure enough the patrol car came by and pulled in ahead of me. When the officer came back I had my license and registration out but he said, "Never mind that. I just wanted to see how many dogs you had in there." Wullie was on the seat beside me, grinning at the cop, and I hauled Rocky and Joe out from under the dash. The cop patted each of them on the head, said, "Better take it easier," and drove off. He was a nice guy, but I think Wullie could have beaten him at gin rummy.

Reprinted from

FIELD & STREAM ~ 1994

Guest Shot: May

By Worth Mathewson

She sleeps that deep, old-dog sleep now. And while she has certainly earned the rest, it makes me sad to watch her. Life is moving so much faster for her now. Those big contagious sleep breaths that my wife refers to as "sleep virus" make me think that the old Lab is just sleeping her way out.

Sometimes I reach down and shake her softly and whisper, "Let's get those ducks, sweetie," then start a series of "quacks." When May was young those quacks were my first real emotional connection with her. I could begin quacking and she would come racing through the house to find me. When she did, she would stand on her hind legs and turn wild circles. She had perfect balance, and could easily have

"Old Lab on Porch" ~ Nigel Hemming

been trained to dance or walk a reasonable distance on her hind legs.

Instead I used those quacks to drive her wild with excitement and happiness. I figured I had reached my goal when she would break from a frenzy of dancing and start tearing around the house in a wild run.

"Take her outside to do that!" my wife would sometimes shout over the quacking and the scratching of the dog nails on the linoleum. But the outside was a scary place for May then, and she didn't dance out there. Not even to quacks.

May is now eleven. I think she aged too fast. She's had tooth problems since youth, and most have now been pulled. She's on a strict diet too, one that includes oatmeal at breakfast, a reduced amount of dry dog food for lunch, and a green vegetable such as green beans or zucchini for supper. Yet she continually implies that she is near starvation. After my wife has fed her lunch, for example, May will wait a bit, then come up to me with her "it's lunchtime" posture. Sometimes I will even get her bowl and start to feed her.

My wife will notice quickly and warn: "That dog is lying to you again; I just fed her."

All our Labs are house dogs. I am convinced that the breed is nurtured by close human contact and is better in the field as a result. We have a big vinyl sofa where dogs are encouraged to sit, and on winter nights with a big fire in the fireplace, the sofa will be filled with humans and Labs.

May's first old-age problem was bladder control, which we have dealt with by letting her out at much more frequent intervals. Also, instead of sitting on the sofa, she now lies next to it in a box padded with old blankets. It's placed where I can reach down and scratch her ears.

We got May from people in Medford, Oregon who were breeding very small Labs. May's mother weighed only 43 pounds, her father, 51. When we got her just after her second birthday May weighed 44 pounds.

May's original name was Maid, but I didn't like it, and changed it. The kennel owner, Val Walker, offered the dog to me for a fraction of the price of other started dogs because she was very nervous and spooky, at times seeming almost uncontrollable. We agreed that I could take her for a season on trial, and if that didn't work I could bring her back and apply the purchase to another dog.

When Val brought May out of her kennel she stayed close to Val's leg. When they came near I squatted, and very carefully May stretched forward to sniff my outstretched hand. Nothing more. Just a timid sniff.

For the drive home, I put her on a blanket on the front seat. I had to lift her in, since she wouldn't go of her own accord. And during the nearly 5-hour drive back she stayed lying down the entire time. We stopped twice for pee breaks and I had to lift her out and in.

After a week both my wife and son felt May should go back to the kennel. The dog's life seemed to be engulfed in terror. I didn't want her living indoors right away, so I'd made a run in the backyard. But within days she had become deathly afraid of her doghouse and wouldn't go near it. During a very hard rain she would just sit, wet, lonely, and scared. I couldn't make her stay in the dryness of the doghouse.

Hunting season opened soon afterwards, and I decided to try her on birds a few times before I made up my mind. For her first field work I took her after band-tailed pigeons in the Coast Range Mountains. There wasn't much of a flight the day we went, so instead we walked the logging roads for ruffled grouse. One flushed, and I folded it with a quick shot. May scurried around in terror, her ears laid back against her head in what my wife came to call the "seal posture."

I don't think she saw the grouse drop. I got her, petted and calmed her down, got her ears back to normal, then took her to the steep, overgrown bank where the grouse had dropped. She smelled something, got interested, worked down the bank, and then very nicely brought the grouse back to hand.

That was when she was two. Until she was about six her life was subject to periods of intense, puzzling terror. For a while she would be almost "normal," then something would throw her into a fit of nerves. At times she would even be afraid to bend her head to eat! The only way we could get food into her was to have me kneel in front of her bowl, then spread my arms much like the wings of a brooding banty hen. Only then would she lower her head to eat.

Certain noises (including her own digestive system) would cause her to rocket up and away, her ears back like a seal's, and a look of terror in her eyes. She didn't bolt when the gun was fired, but she didn't like it, because she would frequently mill around quickly, and didn't always see the bird drop.

But each year got better. The "quacks" from a duck call or my voice seemed to help. By age six she had left most of her terror of the world behind. And then she came into her own, creating memories of triumph—like the time she swam almost out of sight to retrieve a crippled Canada goose on a weather-blown lake, and after what seemed a lifetime, slowly came into sight again, pushing the goose against the strong waves. Or the time she worked some snow-covered sagebrush for 20 minutes and flushed a total of twelve pheasants she alone knew were there.

> And then she came into her own, creating memories of triumph— like the time she swam almost out of sight to retrieve a crippled Canada goose on a weather-blown lake . . .

73

When May started slowing down we got another Lab from Val Walker, a female named Storm Tides, and called Stormy. Val sent us a picture of her as a little puppy that showed her running with a pigeon almost as large as she was.

This is her second season in the field. Last year I took both dogs hunting and deciphered some concern on May's part because Stormy beat her to the retrieves. Then last October both dogs jumped to retrieve a valley quail I had shot. Stormy cleared a barbed-wire fence with an easy leap; May ran into it solidly. She came hobbling back to me, holding one leg straight out. I was sure she had broken it.

I carried her hack to the van and we drove 50 miles to the nearest vet. She hadn't broken anything, but had badly sprained her shoulder. We put the leg in a splint and wrapped the shoulder. It was nearly December before she stopped limping noticeably. Even so, she wasn't happy when I left the house with the gun and Stormy.

This year she doesn't seem to care. Most of the time she is sleeping. Late this summer when I took Stormy down to our pond to cool off and practice retrieving the dummy, May would show some interest. But not much. Pretty soon she would go lie down again.

We are far up in Alberta now. The three of us have been here a couple of weeks.

My wife will fly up in a few days, then we will travel over into Saskatchewan.

For the most part it has been Stormy and me, while May has stayed in the motorhome. On several occasions she has jumped up on the front seats to watch us leave. But when we return she is curled up, very much asleep.

May did come out the other evening to a cut barley field where mallards were coming off a big lake and we were hiding behind rolls of straw. It was good shooting, and I let both dogs go to retrieve. Of course Stormy had the duck and was almost back to me before May got started. After I took the bird from Stormy, I threw it down, and May made a big affair out of retrieving it once again. So I put Stormy on a lead in order to let May bring in the last two ducks. She seemed to enjoy it.

Yesterday I drove past a plowed field with a swathed wheatfield next to it. The plowed field was solid geese; the swathed wheat had over 500 mallards. I found the farmer, who said the plowed field had been peas. The geese were still hopeful about finding some, but the mallards had moved over into the wheat. The farmer suggested it was all right with him if I shot them all.

It has been my experience in prairie Canada grainfields that the birds feed from daybreak until 11 or 11:30, then return to a lake to rest. At about 5:30 or 6 they come to the field again. I told the farmer we would wait until the afternoon flight. He looked with concern to his swathed wheat, totally black with birds.

It was after 3 when I parked the motorhome about a half mile away from the field. A few flocks of ducks were already circling, and some geese had arrived, but the main flock wouldn't come in until after 6.

The situation was perfect for an old dog. And I told her so.

Stormy was in the driver's seat, ears up, intently watching the milling flocks of ducks. May was sound asleep in the passenger's seat, soaking up the rays of the warm afternoon sun.

I knelt beside her, scratched an ear, and called to her quietly. "Come on, let's get those ducks. Quack. Quack. Quack."

Stormy reacted immediately, jumping from the seat and pacing the length of the motorhome expectantly. But I told her no.

I continued talking to May. She was awake and sitting up in the seat. I pointed out the windshield at the ducks

"Let's just you and me go get them. No young dogs invited." She looked out to where I was pointing.

While I gathered my shotgun and other gear May lay back down in the seat. But this time she didn't fall asleep. Stormy watched me closely, her muscles knotted to jump on command. I took her muzzle in my hand and told her that this afternoon was for May. Stormy had her own lifetime of such days ahead.

Of course, when we left without her she didn't understand, didn't like it, and jumped again into the driver's seat to press her nose to the window. May walked closely beside me. After a few yards she seemed to get into the spirit of things. When I went "quack, quack" at her she even made a couple of short sprints in front of me, then stood waiting for me to catch up.

At the field I put down the ground cover, put the decoys around us, and called May. I had her lie down, then stretched out beside her and pulled the ground cover over us. Her eyes were bright. She was starting to watch for birds.

> The situation was perfect for an old dog. And I told her so . . . "Let's just you and me go get them. No young dogs invited."

The limit this year is eight ducks and six Canada geese. Hitting them was no problem because if you stayed under the cover they would light on top of you. First came the mallards—I shot five drakes—and then the geese came. The afternoon was sunny and hot. May was panting heavily from retrieving the ducks, though I had dropped them close. I let the first flock of huge honkers just about settle before throwing the cover back to watch their frantic wingbeats as they reversed direction. It sounded like a helicopter. I shot one with each barrel.

May lurched out to retrieve, but had problems. The first goose had been a cripple and flap-ran almost 100 yards before she was able to catch it. A row of swathed grain, not 10 inches high blocked her path, and when she tried jumping over it with the goose, she stumbled, dropped the bird, and stood panting. I walked over and she immediately reached down to pick the goose up. We walked together to the second goose. She lifted it up to me.

We had other flocks incoming. But I didn't care. May was panting hard and needed a drink that I couldn't give her.

May's panting almost drowned out the sound of incoming ducks and the cries of circling geese. Even so, the birds came right in. But May had finished hunting. She was old, she was tired, and she wanted a drink of water. I gave her a big hug, one from the heart, and while I picked up the decoys, she stretched out. Flocks of geese flared off, honking angrily. The ducks were actually trying to settle as I worked!

Back at the motorhome May drank long and hard. Stormy stood in front, ears perked, watching the ducks circle. This morning May awoke and ate her breakfast of oatmeal. She has been in a deep sleep since.

Reprinted from

FIELD & STREAM ~ 1994

"Just Being Puppies" ~ Nigel Hemming

"There is sorrow enough in the natural way

From men and women to fill our day,

And when we are certain of sorrow in store

Why do we always arrange for more?

Brothers and Sisters, I bid you beware

Of giving your heart to a dog to tear."

—RUDYARD KIPLING

Sweetz's Off-Season

By Jim Fergus

A hunting dog's downtime is for reflection and recuperation—and if there's a goofy young pup around, it's even more fun.

If you're a hunting dog, February is the time of year to take stock of the past season. With months of downtime staring you in the face, many of you field dogs find yourselves getting kind of fretful, if not downright depressed. Depending on where you live, the hunting season is either flat-out over or has only days left to go.

Most of you didn't hunt as much as you might have liked. Sure, your partner made lots of big promises last year. The two of you were finally going to go to South Dakota to hunt those legendary roosters, or maybe take a trip to Montana to chase a "Montana Grand Slam"

"Learning the Ropes" ~ Nigel Hemming

"Humans were denied the speech of animals. The only common ground of communication upon which dogs and men can get together is in fiction."

—O. HENRY, *Memoirs of a Yellow Dog*

(Huns, sharptails, pheasants, prairie chickens). But nooooooo . . .

Your hunting buddy got too busy at work, or on projects around the house, and the kids made demands on his time as kids do. Despite the big talk, all you ended up with was one lousy opening-day trip close to home, where you pottered through a cornfield for a couple of hours, got to flush (or point) a bird or two if you were really lucky and maybe shared one crummy retrieve with a big, out-of-shape, bad-tempered black Lab named Bruno who stole the bird right out of your mouth, threatening to kick your sorry butt if you didn't give it up. Yeah, well, no wonder you're depressed.

"Dog Tired" ~ Kevin Daniel

Of course, some dogs—my yellow Lab, Sweetz, for instance—have chosen their hunting partners a little more carefully. After interviewing dozens of prospective "owners," she cannily picked one who has no kids and is practically professionally obligated to take her out frequently in the field, thereby effectively extending her own hunting season to a full five months or better—starting, say, out West hunting grouse on the first of September and finishing up, for example, in a Florida marsh bagging snipe in the middle of February.

All in all, I think five months is plenty of hunting for Sweetz, who is not as young as she once was and is pretty beat by the end of the season. A dog's pads are a lot like 4x4 truck tires, and hers have a lot of hard miles on them. They've worn thin over the years from scrabbling up rocky talus slopes after chukar and across the volcanic "malpais" rock of the desert, not to mention from countless puncturins by cacti and sandburs. (Some of Sweetz's South Texas hunting-dog pals even have a saying about it: "If it don't bite you, it will stick you or sting you," they say, chuckling among themselves at this knee-slapper . . . uh, tail-wagger.)

By February, Sweetz is not only tired and foot-sore, she's also usually sporting a few new scars from diving through sundry hunting-dog occupational hazards, such as barbed-wire fences. Indeed, Sweetz's whole body has become a kind of road map of our travels and adventures, our seven seasons in the field together. Show me the scar, and I'll tell you the tale of how, when and where it was inflicted. I admit that at the end of her hunting career I won't be able to issue one of those disclaimers they sometimes put in movie credits these days: "No animal was injured in the making of this production."

And this, per-haps, is the downside of being a professional athlete, which is how I think of working hunting dogs. For clearly, in the making of any bird dog, a certain wear and tear is inevitable. This may even shorten the dog's life. Is it worth it? A few years ago I discussed the matter with my vet, for it had occurred to me that I might be wearing out Sweetz's already bad elbows prematurely by hunting her. Maybe she'd be better off staying home. "Only your dog can answer that question," my vet said. "Why don't you ask her?"

So I did. "Okay, would you like to sleep in this morning, or would you rather go hunting?" I now inquire of her regularly. Sweetz has never once during the hunting season elected to stay in bed. In fact, there have been countless times when she has made me get up and go hunting with her when I desperately wanted to sleep in. Indeed, in a real way it is our sporting dogs' genetic programming that encourages us to be hunters.

Still, this year I think Sweetz and I will both feel a little relieved by the time our season comes to an end. For my part, I've got some big plans for the off-season-myriad self-improvement schemes to work on. This is the year I'm really going to work on my shooting. "Yeah, yeah, yeah, I've heard that one before," says Sweetz, who is herself gearing up to spend the long off-season pursuing the Lab's third and fourth favorite hobbies (after hunting and eating): sleeping and taking long, wandering afternoon walks.

In this spirit we were walking on the beach the other day with my fishing guide buddy and hunting companion, Tommy, of Apalachicola, Fla. Tommy has a 10-month-old black Lab named Tango who has all the puppy exuberance, and then some, that I remembered from Sweetz's youth. Seeing the two together, I was never more aware of the fact that Sweetz is, as the golf aficionados say, on the "back nine," with only a handful of hunting seasons left.

We watched as Tango did her impression of a big running English pointer, barreling down the beach until she was just a speck in the distance and then suddenly remembering the rest of us and charging back. She was pure, unformed, unfocused energy, chasing after shore birds, still certain she could catch them, leaping into the sea and dog-paddling Havana-ward after fleeing gulls.

Sweetz, the wise old veteran who figured out a long time ago that she's never going to catch one of these infuriating birds, has given up such nonsense. She apparently thinks herself too mature to have much interest in playing with mindlessly exuberant kids. So she just noodled along, keeping within hunting range, every now and then stepping into a heartbreakingly stiff trot to sniff out a dead fish or any other beached delicacies of the seas (Sweetz's theory is that if isn't old enough and stinking enough to roll in, it's probably at least edible).

She stopped for a moment, looking up to study the upstart's antics with a mildly crotchety regard. Then as if reading my mind, which old dogs are surely capable of doing, Sweetz looked back at me.

"Sure, maybe the kid can run all day," her look seemed to say. "But she doesn't know a damned thing."

Reprinted from

OUTDOOR LIFE ~ 1997

Hot Grits and Blue Yonder

By O. Victor Miller, Jr.

*"That a man's reach should exceed his grasp,
or what's a Heaven for?"*
—BROWNING

*"The only thing more dangerous than a drunk in a pulpwood truck
is a Doctor in a Cessna."*
—UNKNOWN

In a theology class at Mercer University during the 1960's, I was impressed by a quotation by Reinhold Niebuhr in his famous book *Moral Man and Immoral Society*: "Man, unlike other creatures, is both gifted and cursed by an imagination which extends his appetites beyond the requirements of subsistence." I doubt I read the whole book, but that quotation has come home to roost regularly, haunting me all these years, because it accurately describes a fatal flaw of Southern males who lack the wisdom to know what's good for them and the patience to let well enough alone.

"Watch the Birdie" ~ Nigel Hemming

We covet the very things we should avoid. Like Civil wars, high strung bird dogs, and high-tone women who don't go to sleep after an argument. Our imagination extends a fear of falling into a mania for flight, so we neurotically invent angels and buy airplanes. We also attempt quixotically to alter the essential nature of things, dear things like hyperactive bird dogs, somnambulant women, and gravity—although every-body knows it's easier to accept and adjust to those things than to manage them. If there are appropriate maxims to these truths, they are follows: *If God wanted man to fly, he'd been issued wings; don't fall asleep if something's boiling on the stove;* and *seek the wisdom to accept things that can't be changed,* truths which I hope the following parable illustrates.

"Sam is one hardheaded son-of-a-bitch," Frank Wetherbee explained as he buckled the shock collar to his yellow Lab's thick neck. "Which is why I have to turn his collar all the way up." My mastoids ached as I clenched my molars, trying to keep my mouth shut about *hardheaded*. Actually

Sam was a chimera, the rare Labrador retriever who pointed and held birds, although he was inclined to do it as far away as he could get from anybody with a shotgun.

Early shock collars weren't as dependable as the ones you buy now. They didn't have all the bugs ironed out. A low-flying airplane or a hand-held walkie-talkie could set one off. This disjunction conditioned Sam to point birds with his tail between his legs, but I'm getting ahead of myself

Frank got Sam from Ted Baker, a friend who hunts from horseback in north Florida, where the flat open terrain allows Ted to sit his horse and watch dogs work for a country mile. He can stand up in his stirrups and see for another mile. Sam ranged too close for Baker and too far for Wetherbee, which illustrates the same flaw in judgement with which we choose our wives. We marry high strung women and try to settle them down or get us a slow gal and try to soup her up, leaping from one extreme to another instead settling in comfortably on the middle ground.

> **We also attempt quixotically to alter the essential nature of things, dear things like hyperactive bird dogs, somnambulant women, and gravity. . .**

We don't really want what we think we want. And we almost never want what's best for us, a flaw that prompted Frank to get a retriever who ran like a cheetah and try to make him hunt close.

Or take Wayland, a good old boy who sat around the T.V. with popcorn crumbs on his crotch, thumbing through the *Sports Illustrated* bathing suit issue. "Boy!" he said as his imagination extended his appetite beyond the requirements of subsistence. "I bet she could run the fat off my old heart." A month later I saw him walking out of a singles bar with his elbow locked around a teenage myocardial accident looking for a place to happen. A month after that they got married. One day she got to acting ugly, so he turned her over his knee. She pouted about it, which he thought was cute, until he went to sleep and she threw boiling grits on him. There's nothing you can do about boiling grits but scream, that and speed around in your pick-up truck with your face out the window. Molten lava is better than hot grits.

A doctor friend of mine, Streetman Vester, wanted more than anything in the world to fly an airplane. He took lessons for years without ever being able to solo, until finally his instructor told him to give up. Some people aren't meant to fly, and he was one of them. The instructor hated that he'd taken so much money from Streetman, but his conscience wouldn't let him take any more. Dr. Vester trudged sadly off the tarmac, his leather cap clenched in his fist, but before long he found an ultra-light for sale. You don't need a license to fly an ultra-light, a one man apparatus that looks like a beach umbrella with an Elgin outboard motor. I know what he was thinking. If I can't handle a big airplane, I can start with a small one and work my way up—dangerous logic. It's like believing you can handle a small woman or beat up the little guy in a bar. Some very virile things, like viruses, come in small packages. Small women are handy at slinging hot grits or potash syrup after domestic arguments, and little guys can whip your ass before you know it, having collected plenty of experience as first draft choices in barroom brawls.

Dr. Vester bought the ultra-light with a check about the same time Frank brought Sam up from Florida and started gearing him down to a dog he could walk behind. The good doctor found an Oldsmobile dealer with a hanger and a dirt strip in his backyard who was willing to put up with the doctor coming out every Saturday and Sunday to taxi back and forth along the airstrip. So he did. Streetman carried a hand held portable two-way Motorola walkie-talkie to chat with his wife, to advise her of his progress, and to tell her when to have supper hot. Two days every weekend he nearly drove the Oldsmobile dealer crazy with the noise, and the Oldsmobile dealer's wife crazy with red dust. He'd get the ultra-light right up to takeoff speed, reach the end of the runway, shake his head, check in with the Mrs., taxi around and do the same thing over again. He'd beat his fist against his thighs, curse himself for cowardice while something inside him, some subterranean voice that's privy to the wisdom of the ages, whispered, "No, don't do it. Stay on the ground where you belong."

But late one Sunday afternoon just before dusk, he did do it. Not quite intentionally, but with malice aforethought nonetheless. The takeoff was serendipitous, but not inconceivable, since Streetman had been trying to fly an airplane, any airplane, for most of his professional life and had paid out thousands of dollars to flight instructors. You mess with something long enough under the right conditions and you could achieve some small measure of accidental success. Enough monkeys pounding on enough typewriters long enough, still probably won't write *Paradise Lost* but they could hack out a couple columns for *The National Enquirer*. Or like the 80-year-old lawyer's young wife said when she wound up pregnant: "You never know when an old gun's liable to go off."

Anyway, near the end of the strip, the throttle stuck or the doctor hit a bump he hadn't hit before, or a freak gust of head wind puffed him, or maybe his moxie surged, or some rudimentary or atrophied gland squirted hormones into his bloodstream. But miraculously, the airplane bounced off the ground and the physician was airborne before he knew it. Since he'd never had any experience landing, he went ahead and flew. "Wow," he said after he'd cleared his first row of planted pines, "This is—ah—great. I should have done this sooner." After so many jerky stops, starts, and aborted missions, the lift-off was powerfully orgasmic. "Why, oh, why, did I wait so looong?"

Meanwhile, the same Sunday, back on Gravel Hill Farm, Frank and I had finally gotten Sam to range within eyesight, and we succeeded in witnessing an actual point. We'd been pretty sure all along that Sam pointed quail. It's just that we couldn't get close enough to see if any birds got up when he did. Sam or a yellow speck that could have been Sam, was frozen into a crouched and classic rictus two hills over. We'd been jogging all afternoon like Masai warriors, our shotguns at port arms.

As we closed in the last hundred yards, Frank raised his transmitter like the Statue of Liberty, reminding Sam he meant business. Like the doctor's takeoff, we'd worked long and hard to do what we were doing now. Both of us paused, wheezing like a couple of wind broke mules, forty yards from the patch of beggarweed where Sam pointed. "Just look at that!" Frank gasped. "Ain't that the prettiest thing you've ever seen?" Sam was frozen like a concrete dog, the sculpted muscles of his powerful shoulders rigid, his tail pointed toward the darkening sky—where the whisper of the breeze through the longleaf pines slowly gave way to a rising neurotic whine, too high-pitched for a regular airplane. We hardly noticed the doctor's aircraft was getting louder overhead as we approached Sam to honor his point, the doctor's Motorola walkie-talkie or his beeper set off Sam's shock collar. "Kiwi Base, this is Kiwi Bird," he broadcast over the little engine. "I'm airborne, do you read me? Airborne!"

To say Sam busted the covey would be irresponsible understatement. He sprung up on his hind legs, spurting urine and bouncing around in the covey like a pogo stick with flapping ears—AROOO, AROOOP—as the electricity jazzed his blood. The birds flew, not up and out in any common direction to fan out and settle into huntable singles.

They splashed centrifugally outward in all directions from the bouncing dog in wild and whirling flight, sloughing random feathers. Sam bounced like a kangaroo over the last hill of wiregrass and longleaf pines, his front paws never touching the ground. AW, AW, AW, AW!

Frank slapped the control transmitter with his open palm, then threw it down and began stomping it with his boot heel. "What the hell?" he said.

Sam disappeared over one horizon, the doctor's airplane over the other. Of course, I didn't know it was the doctor's airplane until later, just like I didn't know that his walkie-talkie or his beeper set off Sam's collar.

"We sure broke that dog of pointing birds," I said. "Why didn't you shoot?"

"I threw down on that little airplane, but it ducked behind a tree. Why didn't you?"

"I was dodging quail.

Frank and I began hunting Sam, not with him—for him. We looked until dark.

Dr. Vestus soared like an eagle, freed from the corporeal tethers of gravity. He gazed proudly around, purveyor of all that his aquiline eyes could see, from one bruised horizon to the other, one dimly bloodshot by the afterglow of the setting sun. So caught up was he in the miracle of flight, he failed to notice that night had fallen and he was flying around in the darkness somewhere near the Mitchell County line, without running lights or any specific notion of his whereabouts.

When the terrifying reality of his predicament suddenly dawned on him, he decided he'd better land that ultra-light before he ended up on the windshield of a 747. But where? He could distinguish only dark patches and darker patches on the ground. Finally, he mistook a very dark rectangle for a field and went for it, crashing his plane into a stand of planted pines not far from the Mitchell County line. The crash didn't kill him, but it broke up his ultra-light and some bones.

Before the crash Frank and I were still searching for Sam and we might never have found him without a flashlight if the ultra-light hadn't circled back over, setting off the collar again. Of course we couldn't see Streetman but we could hear him screaming, "Mayday, MAYDAY, Mayday? over the mosquito whine of his engine as he passed over, barely clearing the pine tops. Lost people tend to go in circles on land, at sea, or in the air. "What's that fool doing up there flying around in the dark?"

We heard Sam again and found him balled up by a lighterd stump with his paws over his ears, his tongue dirty from dragging in the dirt. Frank dropped to his knees, fumbling the collar off just as the lost doctor circled one last time. YAHHHH! Frank screamed, flinging the shock collar into a tuft of broom sedge, shaking his hands like he'd burned himself with boiling grits. Frank was bent double, his hands sandwiched between his knees. In the darkness I could discern his grimace because his clenched teeth were faintly glowing a luminescent green.

> We heard Sam
> again and found him
> balled up by a lighterd
> stump with his paws over
> his ears, his tongue dirty
> from dragging
> in the dirt.

Then we heard the putter and a whack as Streetman crashed into a stand of planted pines about a mile away. "Serves him right," Frank said.

"Hadn't we better call somebody?"

"We can't call somebody till we get back to the car," he snarled. "Besides, like I said, it serves him right."

We headed back to the kennels, Sam limping gingerly behind us, high-stepping as if he dreaded the idea of grounding himself. His whiskers stayed kinky and the shock collar stayed in the broom sedge.

Dr. Vester lurched around Phoebe Putney Hospital for a while on aluminum crutches, making his rounds with his legs wrapped in plaster. He took up radio controlled model airplanes, which he can crash without bodily investment.

Frank considered bobbing Sam's tucked tail to disguise his lack of temerity. Whenever the poor dog crawls up on a covey of birds, he shimmies like he's stalking diamondback rattlesnakes, and he has slowed down by virtue of the fact that he pauses often to glance in trepidation skyward, proving that even a high strung Labrador retriever can get religion and develop the theological notion that something up there is sitting in judgement with a transmitter or a flaming sword.

Like the rest of us, Sam must live by his instincts, whether he likes it or not. He hunts because it's his nature, but he hunts as though he were also aware of that natural depravity incurred with the original sin, that prelapsarian Fall, when lions stopped lying with lambs and pointers started hunting birds they weren't allowed to eat.

Reprinted with permission from the author

"Dogs are not only a product of their own temperment, but of their owner's as well. You never really train a dog, so much as train the owner."

—Anonymous

Gus and Dinah

By Frederick Busch

Judy and I drove to our new teaching jobs in upper central New York, about 200 miles north of New York City, in a dark blue Corvair convertible. We carried distilled water for the iron, since we thought we were leaving civilization, and we carried a cake Judy had baked for my birthday, which we would celebrate that night, August 1, on the bare floor of the bare apartment we had rented. With us in the car, ears flapping and teeth grinning into the wind that made the Corvair shudder, was Gus, our year-old first Labrador.

Gus helped us celebrate my birthday that night. He also had helped to punctuate the unease that accompanies a big move by chasing the first car he saw in front of our house. He caught it and

"Portrait of Yellow and Black Labs" ~ Nigel Hemming

"Other men saw to the welfare of their dogs from a sense of duty
and business expediency; he saw to the welfare of his as if they were his own
children, because he could not help it."

—JACK LONDON, *For the Love of Man*

it stopped. He somehow sprained a paw and thereafter told the neighborhood of our arrival—it was very late at night—by yelping in an ecstasy of fright and woundedness. That night, the three of us noted my twenty-fourth birthday on the floor of a rented half-house, the furniture for which would come, perhaps, in the morning. Gus ate more of the icing than we did.

He was a wonderful big black dog, with a little soft-fleeced golden retriever in his background. We thought him, as most parents do their first child or surrogate, quite brilliant. We decided at last that he was a writer, perhaps a poet. He was also vindictive, and when we left him once for half a day, alone in the living room, he removed each of three cushions from our sofa, then tore away the lining of the sofa bench and removed every white, wooly wad of stuffing. The living-room floor looked like early snow.

Taking advice from local people, we fetched home a female Labrador who, we were told, would calm our temperamental male. We named her Dinah, and she was as low to the ground, stumpy, whip-tailed and fixed on attending to us—pure Lab, in other words—as Gus was leggy and contemplative.

As they grew into dogdom together, Gus and Dinah acquired a routine. Most mornings, Judy went off to her teaching job at Madison Central School and I left to teach my eight o'clock class of conscripted freshmen. Gus and Dinah left too, for a day's work on the Colgate campus. Gus had no sense of direction that we could discern. He wandered as if lost, often, and we assumed he was either

"I See It!" ~ John Silver

Daniel

perceiving hard or composing about his perceptions. With Dinah on the scene, though, in all her raw bird-dogness, Gus's problems were solved. She headed down Lebanon Street to make a right on Broad and stroll the village green to the campus, and Gus let her lead. He tucked his head along her flank, and they went directly to wherever it was Dinah knew they ought to be. She was the creature of obligations and proprieties, and Gus was, well, he was thinking.

They went, usually, to Taylor Lake, an artificial lake on the edge of the green, hilly campus. We sneaked along on weekend mornings to learn their routine. Dinah made it known to students or faculty that it was her job and Gus's to return to the thrower any tossed object, preferably a stick that would float in Taylor Lake. She brought up the subject by delivering a good-sized piece of wood at the feet of the potential thrower. She stood rigidly, muscles quivering, as if on the

verge of explosion. When the stick was thrown, she followed it. Gus followed her.

At dinnertime, they arrived at the house, Dinah of course in the lead, ready for a meal.

She was also the more nervous about protecting us. We moved to a larger rental house in Hamilton, and we had a backyard. Judy, who loves to garden, knew that we would need a double length of garden hose. We were conscious of what a luxury we had somehow managed to afford, and Judy spent considerable time selecting two lengths of black, heavy hose. We returned with it one Saturday morning, from either Sears or Agway, and we laid it the length of the side driveway, thinking to connect it to the spigot later in the day. In our living room, sitting on the repaired but always lumpy little sofa we'd brought from New York, Judy heard a strange sound—a growling, a kind of tugging, a sound of combat. She asked Gus what he thought it was. He regarded her, checked with me, yawned in dismissal, and returned to his nap.

That afternoon, Judy called me from the house. She had no words. She pointed at the driveway Dinah stood beside her wagging hard: *See? I did it for you.*

Dinah had noted the serpent lying in a dangerous wait, and she had dispatched it. We were saved. The long black menace had been cut apart, sawed by the clean white teeth of a healthy Lab. It lay there, vanquished, in remarkably neat two-foot lengths.

There were generations of their puppies in yards and in dormitories. There were photographs in the student newspaper of Gus and Dinah plunging after sticks in Taylor Lake. Our son Ben came along, and we bought a house in the country where Gus, who lasted longer, was guardian and retriever for Ben and then Nick. He was the resident poet of the house in Poolville.

Our next dog was suburban. We bought him while visiting a friend in Putnam County. We were talking about our current state of doglessness, and she urged upon us the local newspaper. We saw an ad for Labradors, and we—Judy and I and Ben and Nick—fell into instant motion, and were in the car and aiming for a certain downstate kennel. That was where we found Taxi. I named him that because I am from Brooklyn and because we'd just returned from several months in London, and I thought I'd enjoy, each night, calling his name over the cornfield near the Poolville house and

Daniel

evoking a fact of both cities. It was a bellow some of our neighbors never learned to appreciate, and the local dog inspectors were never even approximately charmed.

Taxi became a rural dog promptly enough, and his mission consisted of allowing children to play with and on him, and of killing snakes in Judy's garden with a fervor one associates with the mongoose.

In nearby Poolville Lake, where Judy and the boys were picnicking one afternoon, Taxi saw a deer in the brush. He made sounds of confusion and pursuit, and the deer leaped into the lake to swim for its life. Taxi followed, and he became part of our own wonderful version of Keats's urn: the deer forever in frantic retreat—doing, it would have to be said, a version of dog paddle and Taxi forever in pursuit to the tune of his panting and wet groans. We are required, by fondness and perversity, to once in a while wonder what he might have done had he caught the deer.

Now there are Junior and Jake. Taxi lived long enough to show the precincts to Jake, a small, purebred male who is the loyalest of friends. And Jake has in turn shown Junior, a year younger than he and a good deal larger, how to patrol the acres around the house where we now live, on a wild ridge above Sherburne, New York.

Jake is quite reminiscent of Dinah, and Junior is shaggy and not unlike Gus. It is Junior who eyes the hoses with Dinah's slightly mad glare, and it is Junior who has retrieved small rabbits and baby birds. Jake is awash in being dutiful. He delivers hurled sticks or balls with solemn urgency, while Junior, once he has retrieved them, is content to chew them into neat segments.

Each is a handsome, funny companion and each is our friend. And neither's the poet Gus was.

Reprinted from

DOG PEOPLE ~ 1995

"Three's Company" ~ Kevin Daniel

Tale of a Pup

By Robert F. Jones

EXCERPT FROM GUNNING DIARY

Date: 31 Oct. 1989, Tuesday, 12:30-2:00 p.m., 17th day afield.

Area: Shatterack Mountain, from Danny's apples to Ray's red pines.

Dogs: Luke, 11-year-old black Lab; Jake, 11-week-old yellow Lab puppy.

Weather: High 60s, rain in a.m., overcast, light SW breeze, occ. showers.

Gun: 20-gauge Winchester Model 23 double, low-base #9 shot.

Flushes: 2 grouse, 1 woodcock.

Shots: 1 at one woodcock; bagged.

Running total: 63 flushes in 26 hours afield (33 grouse, 30 woodcock); 22 shots fired at 18 birds, 11 bagged (3 grouse, 8 woodcock). Batting .500!

"Yellow and Black Lab Pups" ~ Nigel Hemming

"His puppyhood was a period of foolish rebellion. He was always worsted

but he fought back because it was his nature to fight back.

And he was unconquerable."

—JACK LONDON

Remarks: Luke pushed a grouse uphill through the pine-and-birch thicket across from Canary Brook and flushed it at the edge of the clearing at top. Bird went out too low for a shot. We followed across through thin woods toward Danny's old apple orchard, where the grouse seemed to have pitched in. Luke ranged ahead, looking for a reflush. Jake stayed with me, about five yards ahead, his fat puppy belly plastered with mud (some of which scraped off when he dragged it over fallen tree trunks), his outsized paws scrabbling energetically in the muck for traction. About halfway to the apples, a woodcock went off under Jake's nose, twittering like a windup toy, angling L to R almost straightaway. I popped it about 20 yds. out. Jake saw it fall—heard it thump down—then instinctively raced for it, his ears flapping like limp yellow wings. Luke, too, had heard the shot and seen the bird fall and saw Jake run for the retrieve. Luke beat Jake to the woodcock—outraged at the puppy's act of lèse majesté—and picked it up in the nick of time. Luke looked straight at me, as if to say, How *could* you?—and then deliberately *crunched* the bird! Sibling rivalry? You bet. But it was Jake's first bird. . . .

Good gundogs have this in common with the best of human athletes: They improve with age, up to a point. Just as a fighter—Ray Leonard, for example—compensates for waning hand speed with greater ring savvy, or an aging quarterback overcomes the lack of mobility imposed by brittle knees with a keener reading of defenses, so too does a wise old bird dog beat the slows with the smarts. Maybe you can't teach an old dog new tricks, but if he's any good, he sure can teach himself.

My grizzled black Labrador, Luke, did just that over the course of a career spanning 11 splendid upland bird seasons. In his youth he was likely to forget me in the ecstasy of the hunt, following his nose over hill and dale after hot, heady bird scents and flushing woodcock or grouse well out of range. By our fifth season together—he would have been 35 human years old by that time and already slowing down—I began to notice that he was not only working closer to the gun, but flushing more birds than ever directly back to me. At first I thought it was a fluke, but I began to keep stats on him. In the past six seasons, Luke has flushed a total of 1,078 birds (567 woodcock, 511 ruffed grouse); 63% of them have flown toward or past my gun.

I can tell you when he's getting "birdy": His strong otterine tail comes up and starts flailing faster; his brown eyes flash over to me, whenever I'm moving through the cover, and we make what they call in the singles bars "meaningful eye contact"; his thick coat, shiny already, seems to light up from within and throw blue-black glints as his hackles rise. He will circle out beyond the

102

bird, then rush in, whuffling and gulping the delicious scent, and more often than not, the bird flushes my way. Then it's up to me. (I would like to say my batting average is as good as Luke's flush-back percentage, but it's not. Over the past four seasons, I've hit only 37.5% of the birds I've shot at.) When I miss, Luke looks back at me with doleful eyes and seems to shake his head. All that work for nothing.

When I connect, though, he's in his element—retrieving. Sharp-eyed, he marks the bird down and leaps after it. Into muddy swamp edges, barbed thickets of multiflora rose, doghair aspen or maple brakes, through ice-edged rushing brooks, even a few times into deep snowdrifts. Luke always gets his bird. If it's down, it's ours. Even if the bird, most often a grouse, is only wing-tipped and running, Luke goes after it like a four-legged Edwin Moses, sometimes for as far as a quarter of a mile, and brings it back proudly but gently to drop it at my feet.

Two seasons ago we were working through a patch of old apple trees for grouse. At the far end Luke got birdy in some whippy stuff and pushed out a woodcock. I fired just as it turned a corner around a big maple tree that was still in full leaf. It seemed to me I was behind the bird and that I had missed it. The afternoon was hot, and we were both breathing so hard, so I told Luke, "Let's take a break." He seemed reluctant, but he sat, edgy, muttering, eager. Ten minutes later we pushed on, around the maple tree where I'd fired at the woodcock. Luke stopped about five yards behind me, looked at the ground, then looked up at me quizzically. "Come on," I said, a bit sharply. "Hunt 'em up, hunt 'em up!" Again he seemed to shake his head, again looked at the ground before him. I went back to where he stood. There lay the woodcock I had shot at 10 minutes earlier. "O.K.," I said, embarrassed. "Fetch." He fetched and gave, the ritual complete. I never loved him more. We hunted on. . . .

But time—"that old bald cheater," as Ben Jonson called it— deals down and dirty with all of us. As the 1989 bird season neared, I realized that Luke would have to hang up his bell collar pretty soon. His left shoulder was arthritic, the bounce was fading from his rear suspension, and his eyes were growing hazy-blue with incipient cataracts. After all, he was 11 years old—77 in human terms. I could handle the arthritis by feeding him an aspirin wrapped in raw hamburger before we went out each day; the spring would return to his stride as the season wore on and he put more up-and-down miles behind him; his nose would make up in keenness for what his eyes had lost. More disconcerting was a new problem: Over the winter and spring, he had developed a hacking, half-strangulated cough that wouldn't go away. His bark sounded broken, like a teenage boy's voice when it's changing; his breath came raspy at the best of times. Jean Ceglowski, our sure-handed local vet, X-rayed Luke's chest and throat.

"Laryngeal hemiplegia," she said once she had studied the results. "Half of his bark box—his larynx—is paralyzed. Nobody knows what causes it, but it happens, most commonly in racehorses. They call them 'roarers.' I'll give you something for it, a cortisone-based drug called prednisone. Just a five-milligram pill every other day. It can't cure it, but at least it'll relieve the inflammation, make it easier for him to swallow."

"Can I hunt him?"

"Sure," she said, tousling Luke's ears as he looked up gravely at her. Jean often rode her own horses near coverts we hunted on, a wild, wooded ridge just back of town. Sometimes she would tell me where she had seen grouse dusting or feeding. She knew what Luke was made of—all heart. "Bird hunting,"

she told him now. "That's what you live for, isn't it?" His ears perked, and his tail thumped, *Yes, indeed!*

But clearly, and sadly, it was time to start looking for a replacement dog. If life were fair, hunters and their gundogs would have identical life spans—learning, peaking and declining together, step for step, one man, one dog hunting along together on a trail toward that Great Grouse Covert in the Sky—but it doesn't work that way. As if in compensation, though, the Good Lord of Upland Gunning sometimes takes pity on hunters and throws good fortune our way. No sooner had I decided to seek a puppy than my friend Dan Gerber called from Michigan. A fine poet, novelist and onetime sports car racer—he drove Cobras and Mustangs, often for Carroll Shelby, until a 100-mph meeting with a wall at Riverside (Calif.) International Raceway in 1966 convinced him that words were gentler than wheels—Dan had recently endured what I would have to face in a year or two. He had had to put down his dearest old dog, Lily, a 13-year-old yellow Labrador who had figured powerfully and poignantly in many of his writings.

"I've backtracked Lily's bloodlines," Dan told me, "and located a yellow Lab female who's going to whelp in mid-August. She's the spitting image of Lily—same gentle

> If life were fair, hunters and their gundogs would have identical life spans.

disposition—and the puppies will be ready for weaning in early October. You want one?"

Dan hadn't hunted Lily as hard as I hunt my dogs, though the few times we had been out with her together she looked keen enough. You certainly couldn't fault her intelligence and what dog men call "biddability"—the eagerness to please and learn. And she was one of the gentlest, calmest, most affable dogs I had ever known—save Luke, of course. "Damn right I want one," I said.

Done and done. Now all that remained was to drive to Dan's place to collect the pup, a 900-mile trip from my home in southwestern Vermont to his in western Michigan. I took off bright and early one morning in October, accompanied by a good-hearted pal, Sean Donovan, from nearby Salem, N.Y. By alternating at the wheel of my GMC Jimmy, we would make the trip in one shot, on interstates or high-speed highways almost the entire distance, with plenty of coffee and conversation to keep us cooking.

It devolved into a virtually nonstop monologue on my part, about the gundogs in my life to date. Sean, not a bird hunter but a gentleman nonetheless, distinguished himself as a good listener. He heard more than he probably cared to—about Rusty and Belle, the neighborhood Irish setters who had picked me up after school during my boyhood in Wisconsin and led me into virgin woods and fields after prairie chickens, sharp-tailed grouse, woodcock, snipe, mourning doves, ruffed grouse and big, gaudy ring-necked pheasants (the glamour birds of my youth) that would erupt off the ground, cackling like airborne alarm clocks when the setters double-teamed them and put an end to their raucous escape plans.

Later after I had married and moved to New York, there was Peter, my first black Lab, raised from a puppy to hunt the woods and overgrown meadows of Westchester County. But Peter disappeared before his time. Dog-nappers had been working the area, my wife, Louise, and I learned too late, and I suspect they trolled Peter into a van, using a bitch in heat as bait. Bitter and disconsolate over the loss, I vowed that my next dog would live in a kennel except when he was out hunting with me.

German shorthaired pointers were all the rage then—the mid-1960s—and Max was a superb specimen. He could cover a 20-acre meadow like a supersonic vacuum cleaner, lock on point and hold it as solidly as a bridge pier, mark a bird down in the thickest of cover and fetch it back—most of the time—undented by canine teeth. One bleak, windy November afternoon, we choused a solitary quail out of a stonewall covert. I fired when it had cleared the tree line, saw it fold and fall. I sent Max to fetch, then followed up when he didn't return in his usual 10 seconds. I found him sniffing all around for the bird, to no apparent avail. After 20 minutes or so, I called him off and we hunted on. Then, after about an hour, I noticed that Max's cheek was swollen. He must have cut it on some rusty barbed wire, I thought, and called him over to examine it. He was reluctant to come.

"Yellow Lab with Two Pups" ~ Nigel Hemming

"Get over here!" He came in, slinking and avoiding my eyes.

"Sit!"

I turned his head to look at the cheek. My god, a growth had sprouted from the corner of his mouth! I looked again and saw . . . the head of a quail, peeking out at me, all covered in saliva.

"Give, Max."

He spit the wounded bird out, then sneaked away shamefacedly. He had collected the quail I knocked down, all right, then kept it hidden in his mouth, sucking it for more than an hour, savoring it, like a feathery jawbreaker.

But good as he was in the field, Max just wasn't a Labrador. A one-man dog, he was surly with visitors, hated kids, and because he had been raised in the kennel I built for him and lived most of the time outdoors, was never housebroken—which made for some ugly scenes when I would go soft and invite him inside during subzero weather.

So we acquired another Lab—a yellow one this time, three years old when we gladly took him off the hands of a British couple who were moving back to England. His name was Simba (leave it to the Brits to name a dog for a cat) and he was truly leonine in both size—105 pounds, with a head like a pale gold anvil—and dignity.

For a few years I hunted Max and Simba as a team, pointer and flushing retriever, and was in bird-dog heaven. Max would hunt the overgrown fields and thickets to my right, while Simba coursed the brush-grown stone walls to my left. But Max, at the age of five, contracted heartworm, then virtually unknown in the Northeast (though endemic in the South). We took him to three vets before one of them diagnosed it, but too late. He fought, hard and valiantly, but one foggy spring morning I woke just at dawn and knew he had lost. I went down to where I had bedded him in the kitchen, stared at him for a while, cold there on the linoleum floor, then wrapped him in his blanket for the last time and tried hard not to cry. With him died my interest in owning pointers. I would be a Labrador man from then on.

Why, you might ask (and many have), would a dedicated upland bird hunter prefer a Lab to the more surefire pointing breeds? Wouldn't a more traditional dog like

> There's a kind of existential quality to pounding along fast behind your dog, seeing it get birdy, tail going like mad . . . It all happens so fast.

an English setter or pointer, a German shorthair or a Brittany spaniel—actually the dog of choice in my part of New England—produce more birds for you? Of course it would, but not the way I liked to hunt them. I certainly admire the control and walking-on-eggs caution a good pointing dog exercises in its craft, but I'm not out for a high body count. I much prefer the spontaneity of hunting behind a flushing dog. There's a kind of existential quality to pounding along fast behind your dog, seeing it get birdy, tail going like mad, then checking back to see that you are ready before the dog will plunge in to flush the bird. It all happens fast. You learn to shoot from any position. You may not get as many shots or hit as many birds, but you never lose any cripples.

And, anyway, I just love Labs. . . .

At first glance, at least, the puppy that waddled toward me the next day, grinning and flailing its short, thick tail so violently that it threatened to wag itself off its pins, was as lovable as they come—but he looked more like a furry piglet or a blond bear cub than a registered, blue-blooded Labrador retriever with the high-flown name of Toynton's Kent Hollow Jake. His sister, whom Dan Gerber had dubbed Toynton's Willa (after Willa Cather), looked just the same.

The breeders, a gracious couple named Grace and Myron Morris of Zeeland, Mich.,

had asked us to choose names for the pups soon after they were born, so that by the time we picked them up eight weeks later, they would respond when called. They did.

Sean and I had arrived at Dan's lakeside home north of Fremont, Mich., at midnight, then drove the 40 or so miles south to Zeeland the next morning in Dan's Range Rover to collect the pups. "They're clever little rascals," Grace Morris said. "Real quick to learn." With the pups at our heels, we had gone down to the big kennels behind the Morris house to have a look at Jake and Willa's sire, Shamrock Acres Reign Maker, more familiarly known as Dewey. He proved to be a massive, friendly yellow with wide-set eyes in a large head. "He weighs 100 pounds," Grace said, "with not a speck of fat on him." The pups' dam, Millie (more formally, Toynton's Millicent After Six), was smaller, of course, but similarly equable in disposition. She was a bit brusque with the pups, though, when they dived at her still-sagging and red-chawed dugs for a now-illicit snack. "There were only three puppies in the litter," Grace told us, "two male and one female. The other male, Hogan, left yesterday with his new owners." Sean, who had perked up at the news that there was third pup in the litter, looked a

"A Day at the Races" ~Michael Jackson

bit downcast. "Damn," he told me later, "if I'd known how great they were, I'd have put in with you for one of them."

Grace had baked some bread and chocolate chip cookies, so over coffee and cookies in her kitchen, with the pups fussing at our feet, we listened to feeding, health and training suggestions. "I'd appreciate it if you'd keep in touch," Grace said. "Send me a note on their progress and a picture now and then. These dogs will mean a lot to you, I know, but they mean a lot to me, too."

"Come on," Dan said to me, grinning behind his bushy mustache. "I want to get home and roll around on the floor and chew on our puppies."

We did just that, then took Jake and Willa for a long walk through the beech woods surrounding Dan's house. The pups staggered, flopped, fell over twigs, jumped on each other in ambush, splashed joyfully through every muddy puddle along the way, and in general fulfilled all the puppy clichés, but they kept up. At one point a ruffed grouse blew out of a downed pine tree about 50 yards ahead of us. They looked up at the roar of the bird's wings, but clearly they couldn't focus that far ahead yet. "It'll come in time," I said. Dan nodded, then got down on his knees in the mud and regarded the pups. "I would like to compliment the both of you," he told them solemnly. "Your puppy disguises are perfect. You have every last mannerism down to a tee. I believe you're fully prepared now for your secret mission." The pups waggled their outsized heads joyfully, then Willa leaped on Jake and knocked him flat in a mud puddle.

The pair of them slept well that night, their last together for quite a while. Grace had warned us that the pups woke up at 5:30 a.m. sharp, "regular as an alarm clock, goldarn it," and early the next morning—after a hearty breakfast of puppy chow (for Jake) and a quick perambulation in the woods—Sean and I bundled Jake into the travel kennel in the back of my Jimmy and headed back east. The pup surprised us by not fussing a bit on separation from the last of his littermates. With occasional pit stops for feeding and piddle breaks, the return trip was painless for all hands.

Louise and our menagerie—Luke plus three cats (one a four-month-old kitten)—were waiting when I wheeled into the barnyard at 2 a.m. the next day. Jake was the object of all eyes (and noses). Louise oohed and aahed and cuddled. Luke sniffed the pup from stem to stern, wagged his tail halfheartedly, then walked away indifferently: What else is new? The two older cats, Sam and Ninja, took one look at the newcomer, hissed in loud feline horror, and headed for the hills, where they remained for the better part of the next two weeks.

The kitten, Spike Jones, welcomed Jake rapturously, like a long-lost brother. Louise, a sucker for baby animals (as am I), had acquired Spike in August while I was fishing for brook trout in Canada. He had been received coolly, to say the least, by the adult pets. Luke, always easygoing, allowed Spike a few liberties, such as letting the kitten cuddle against him while both of them snoozed, but when Spike tried to play floor hockey with

Luke's tail, he growled ominously. Sam eventually permitted the kitten to walk within easy striking range, even brush against him, but when Spike essayed a little kittenish roughhouse—for example, quick, claw-sheathed left jabs at Sam's beezer—the old neutered tom merely slammed the kitten to the floor and stalked disdainfully away. Upon her return, Ninja, who brooks no familiarities from anyone of any species or any size, slapped the kitten silly the first time she realized that Spike was living with us permanently, and every time thereafter when he so much as walked into the same room with her. The message was clear, and Spike heeded it. (And heeds it to this day, though he's twice Ninja's size.)

As soon as Jake entered the household, however, he and Spike were playmates and pals. Young drawn to young, and about the same size, though Jake, of course, was heavier. They raced at one another, embraced on their hind legs, and immediately began mouth wrestling. The clumsy yellow puppy and the agile black-and-white kitten zoomed around the house like piebald chain lightning. Jake loved nothing more than to take Spike's entire head into his mouth and seemingly—to our initial horror—gnaw on it like a soup bone. Or he would grab Spike by a hind paw, chew his toenails, then drag the kitten around for a while.

Conversely, when Jake flopped down for one of his instant, quarter-hourly naps, Spike would stalk him as a lion might a buffalo, then spring on the pup in midsnore, deliver a dozen snake-quick blows to the

"Puppies and Puddle" ~ John Silver

head and split for cover before Jake knew what had happened. Spike's favorite hide-outs were under the coffee table and beneath the skirted hassock of my favorite living room chair. There he would lurk until Jake clumped by, at which point a razor-tipped paw would dart out and zap Jake's hocks. While Jake tried to snuffle into the hideaway, the kitten would escape out the other side. At which point the game would be repeated ad infinitum, much to the dis-composure of the rest of the household.

Whenever I drove into town, I made it a point to take Jake with me. That way, I reasoned, his easygoing familiarity with motor travel, well-learned on the long drive back from Michigan, would remain intact. One of Luke's few drawbacks was that whenever I took him with me in the truck, he reckoned we were heading for a grouse cover, so he would get "up" for it—yelping, shivering, now and then breaking into a querulous, barely controlled yowl that threatened to rupture my eardrums. I certainly couldn't fault him for eagerness, but it was embarrassing—especially when the neighbors half a mile down the road told me they could always tell by the accompanying sound effects when I was going out hunting.

Jake stayed calm, though, and I discovered another unsuspected benefit to taking your puppy with you while running errands: Good-looking women, who wouldn't have looked

twice at an old geezer by his lonesome, now stopped to chirp and coo over the puppy. "He's just *adorable!*" they would croon, then gaze up at me with soft, loving eyes. When I rather bashfully reported this phenomenon to my wife, she gazed up at me and said, with a soft, knowing laugh: "What do you expect? Good-looking guys say the same thing when I've got him with me."

So young Jake was accommodating very nicely to our domestic situation. It remained to be seen, however, how well he would adapt to his primary role as gundog and heir to the exemplary Luke. I couldn't expect Jake to develop into a "finished" hunting dog in just one season, certainly not with him starting this young in life. All of my earlier dogs had been born in the spring, so that by the time they first went afield with me the following fall, they were at least five months old. I had never started a puppy this young before, but I knew that at least I could determine if he had the makings. And I hoped that just by tagging along in company with Luke, he might get a glimmer of what it was all about.

The first step in the pup's education was to get him used to gunfire. The day after we arrived back from Michigan, Sean and his seven-year-old son, Richard, came over to help me. While Richard held Jake on a leash about 30 feet away, Sean threw clay pigeons for me from a foot trap. I popped them with a 20-gauge. Jake not only didn't flinch or seem frightened in the least by the noise, he appeared positively overjoyed by it. Richard brought him closer as I shot six clay birds in a row, and at the end he was sitting directly under the muzzle of the gun. A good start.

That afternoon I took Jake with me while Luke and I hunted the cover behind my house. It was sunny and brisk, with a light northwest wind, and a frost the previous night had the maple leaves falling like giant golden snowflakes. Jake trotted along right at my heels, his brand-new collar bell jangling, while Luke quartered ahead of us, staying within shooting range. About a half mile up the woods road, Luke flushed a woodcock that flew out straight down the trail—a lead-pipe-cinch shot, which I missed. With both barrels. I would like to say I was distracted by the puppy being underfoot, but it was just plain lousy shooting. Still, Jake seemed to see the bird get up and intently watched it fly away, at least as far as he could focus.

We flushed two more birds—grouse—on the way back in, but the cover was still too thick to see either of them, and I didn't shoot. All told, we were out an hour and a quarter, and Jake seemed ready for a nap. I left him at home while Luke and I went to another cover, where I killed two woodcock. When we got home, just before dark, Jake was awake. I let him sniff one of the dead birds. He stared at it for a moment, then glommed it with a growl. Later, I let him worry one of the wings while I cleaned the birds, so he could get the taste of it. He mouthed it quite gently, with the inborn caution of any baby confronting something new, and I reinforced him with encouraging words. When he got bolder and started to chomp down on the wing, I distracted him and "disappeared" it, then quickly got him into the house where Spike was waiting to distract him further.

In my gunning diary for that day, I wrote: "Jake's first day afield. Not gunshy, not afraid of the woods, ready to run with Luke when Luke will let him. Doesn't dislike the smell or taste of woodcock—indeed, he's keen for them. Didn't whine or sulk when I'd inadvertently clipped his jaw as he followed on my heels. Motored over and under logs & through mud & streams quite manfully—as if it were old stuff for him. Came when I called or whistled to him. All told, looks quite hopeful."

Over the next three weeks Jake logged many woodsy miles on his ever stronger legs. He hunted through warm weather and cold, through sun, rain, sleet and once the beginnings of a thunderstorm. He met other denizens of the woods: rabbits, songbirds, a pileated woodpecker, a flock of wild turkeys and many, many deer. Because Luke did not chase them if they ran from us,

> Over the next three weeks Jake logged many woodsy miles on his ever stronger legs.

"All in a Day's Work" ~ Nigel Hemming

and the gun's loud voice didn't speak, Jake learned that they weren't what we were after. He saw or sensed when Luke got excited over fresh grouse or woodcock scent, saw or heard me shoot when shootable birds got up, watched Luke run in and make the retrieve, and envied the praise I gave the older dog for his performance.

Jake still hadn't put it all together, but he was getting the gist of it. He knew already that when I pulled on my boots and shooting vest, we were getting ready for something special. He knew that when I buckled on his extra collar—the one that went *clang, clang, clang* when he was wearing it—the moment was near. And he knew that when I brought the shotgun down from the gun cabinet, the moment was indeed right now. In his brief life, that was approximately doggy heaven.

But it wasn't until the 17th day afield, a forever memorable October afternoon, that it all clicked into place. Well, most of it. Certainly I'll never forget that overcast, rather muggy day, with the woodcock suddenly erupting under Jake's inquisitive nose, with me bringing the gun to my shoulder instinctively and centering the bird as it dodged away at speed, yet still aware out of my peripheral vision of Jake's eyes locked on it as it flew, hitting the trigger and seeing the bird puff and fall and bounce on the leaf-strewn ground—and Jake quivering for an instant, then lining out as fast as his puppy legs would carry him towards the fallen prey.

But as my diary records, Luke got there first and asserted his rights as Number One

Dog—still. He made it clear to us both that a dog had his dignity, even if his day was fast waning. Jake honored that right (what other choice did he have?), and I honored it as well, allowing Luke the retrieve on all the birds we killed together through the remainder of that season. Some of the retrieves were tough, and I hoped that by hanging back with me as we watched Luke make them, Jake would learn something. One bird fell in what seemed an impossible tangle of multiflora rose briars that had grown up amidst a jungle of aspen tops left behind by loggers. Luke hadn't seen the bird fall—he was off to the side when it flushed back over his head— and had to respond to my hand signals to find the spot. When he figured out where I was sending him, he looked up at me as if to say, "You want me to go in *there?*" Then a fluke of the breeze brought him scent of the downed bird. His ears perked and his tail went up. "O.K., you're the boss!" And in he dived, to emerge five minutes later with bloody ears and tail—and the bird between his jaws. He dropped the grouse at my feet, then sat and looked up at me, grinning. That's what it's all about.

The pup sat at my feet, staring up at his black teacher, with a quizzical look. Oh, I get it, he seemed to be thinking. If it flies, it dies. And if it dies, it *fries!*

It's now a year later, and Jake is bigger than Luke—a full head taller and 80 pounds to the older dog's 65. He'll probably top out at 95 to 100 pounds when he fills out in the chest and haunches. I'm amazed at how much he learned from Luke in his puppy season: He works close and enthusiastically on grouse and woodcock, but when his enthusiasm carries him beyond gun range, he returns without hesitation to two blasts on the Acme Thunderer whistle.

I took him down to Maryland's Eastern Shore earlier this fall for his first outing on ducks: He sat quivering against me in the blind, steady to the roar of shotguns when the birds tolled in to the decoys, then retrieved from the water—through thick weeds, a high wind and breaking waves on the bay— responding well to the hand signals he had learned when he couldn't see the dead birds. He brought in 25 ducks, dead and cripples, and didn't crunch a one. Nor has he yet mangled an upland bird, though he has a tendency to pick up wounded woodcock by a wing and toss them into the air, then catch them gently in his mouth as they fall.

My only disappointment with him came last spring, when I tried to make a fishing dog out of him. Simba, my first yellow Lab, used to accompany me on the trout streams, holding at heel while I threw the fly,

watching carefully as I played a fish, then picking the fish up at leader length without ruffling a scale and bringing it to my hand. But Jake thought that the whole point of the exercise was to retrieve the fly, and when I would whisk it away from him to prevent his getting hooked, he would run back along the bank, shake water all over me and jump at my head just for fun.

He also enjoyed charging upstream ahead of me, flushing trout out of their lies and turning them to run madly between my legs. Great technique on grouse, a disaster on brookies. Jake's a laugh a minute on a trout stream.

But he already has a way with the ladies. In the course of our travels, he has received two proposals of doggy matrimony, one from the owner of a high-bred young yellow Lab female in Maryland, and the other from a damsel in Georgia whose owner offered to pay Jake's airfare down there for the nuptials. When my friend Jim Fergus dropped in this fall from Idaho for a few days of Eastern upland shooting, he brought Sweetzer, his two-year-old yellow Lab female, with him. Jake was smitten, chasing her around the yard for half an hour, then further showing his affection by knocking her flat with a shoulder block. The two of them eventually settled down for a quiet game of tug-of-war with a convenient maple branch. Unfortunately, Sweetz had already been spayed, so their friendship remains perforce platonic.

Meanwhile, old black Luke has gotten a new lease on life. Last spring, at Jean Ceglowski's suggestion, I took him north

119

to Burlington, Vt., where Dr. Paul Howard, a veterinary surgeon, performed throat surgery on him. Howard removed Luke's paralyzed vocal folds, and thus opened a wider passage in his larynx so he could breathe more easily. When I picked Luke up the next day, he seemed five years younger, and although arthritis still bothers him, he hunted almost as well as ever this fall.

The only trouble is that now I have to keep my eyes focused on two close-working flushing retrievers at once, and on two occasions they both put up woodcock at roughly the same time, about 15 yards apart. I missed both birds, both times.

Too much of a good thing? I'm not complaining.

Reprinted from

SPORTS ILLUSTRATED ~ 1990

"Sole Mates" ~ Kevin Daniel

Example

I want my boy to have a dog,
Or maybe two or three—
He'll learn from them much easier
than he would learn from me;
A dog will show him how to love,
And bear no grudge or hate—
I'm not so good at that myself,
But dogs will do it straight.
I want my boy to have a dog
To be his pal, and friend;
So he may learn that friendship sticks—
Is faithful to the end.
And if I should select a school
To teach my boy to live—
I'd get a pair of pups for him
That had these things to give.
There never yet has been a dog
Who learned to double-cross—
Nor catered to you when you won,
Then dropped you when you lost,
To teach my boy of friendship's worth,
I'll never sign him up
With any school that ever was—
I'll just buy him a pup.

—MARTY HALE, *The Old Spinner*

"Best Friends" ~ Kevin Daniel

Labs to the Rescue

Four True Stories of Animal Courage and Kindness
By Kristen von Kreisler

On a freezing winter day, Sean Lingl and his friend Danny Parker rowed a small plastic dinghy across the mouth of the Nimpkish River on British Columbia's Vancouver Island. Rain poured down, and wind roughened the water, tossing the dinghy about as if it were a thimble. But the men, eager to get to an island just off the coast, kept rowing.

Lingl's chocolate Labrador retriever Tia sat shivering in the boat between them. Not immediately obvious from the angle of her sitting position was the harsh reality that she had only three legs. Four years before, as she'd chased Lingl's truck down a gravel road, she'd run into a ditch and cut her right hind paw on a broken bottle. Her veterinarian

"Veterans" ~ Nigel Hemming

"There is no faith which has never yet been broken
except that of a truly faithful dog."

—KONRAD LORENZ, *King Solomon's Ring*

treated the injury, but infection set in and spread up her leg.

"I'll have to amputate it," the vet told Lingl. "I have no choice."

Lingl thought of putting her down. He did not want her hobbling, crippled, through life, with people wincing and pitying her. But the vet persuaded him to let Tia have the surgery. Afterward, her indomitable spirit convinced Lingl that he had been right to let her live.

As the wind blasted water into the dinghy, Lingl did not worry. The boat's double plastic hull created a pocket of air that would hold the boat up, no matter how much water filled it, he told Parker. They were in no danger unless a hole was somehow punctured in the outer layer. A hole would let water into the pocket and sink the boat.

When they began tilting farther and farther to one side, however, Lingl did start to worry. "Something's not right," he said. "Maybe we should go back."

"Let's do it," Parker agreed.

As they turned the boat around and headed toward shore, the wind flipped the

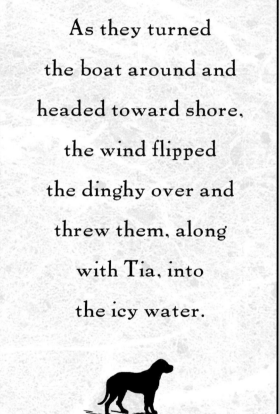

As they turned the boat around and headed toward shore, the wind flipped the dinghy over and threw them, along with Tia, into the icy water.

dinghy over and threw them, along with Tia, into the icy water. The men sputtered, shivering violently. To keep their heads above water, they clung to the side of the capsized boat.

"Where's Tia?" Lingl shouted.

He groped for her and found her trapped under the dinghy. Grabbing her by the fur, he pulled her out and set her free. Even with only three legs, at least she'd have the chance to swim ashore and save herself.

Lingl and Parker were not going to be so lucky. The cold itself was cause for alarm: They could not survive in this water for long. Even worse, they both were wearing heavy boots and chest waders, firmly attached by belts and suspenders. If the waders continued filling with water, Lingl and Parker would sink like anchors. And there was no help in sight.

Lingl pulled himself up just enough to see over the boat. He figured that they had to cross about a hundred yards of freezing waves to reach shore . . . and only a few minutes to do it before they sank or died from exposure. They were looking death in the face, and they knew it.

Then Lingl suddenly noticed that the boat was moving toward the beach. Amazed, he looked around to discover the source of this miraculous motion. Tia had gripped the dinghy's mooring rope between her teeth and, with her three legs, was swimming with every ounce of her strength and pulling the boat to safety.

Astounded by her courage, Lingl and Parker helped her move the boat along by kicking even in their chest waders. Though the wind slapped huge waves in the water and tossed Tia as if she were a cork, she gritted her teeth around the rope and paddled as hard as she could to keep from going under. Blinking against the stinging salt, she battled the waves until she'd pulled Lingl and Parker to water shallow enough for them to stand. She let go of the rope as they staggered to shore.

The men's hair turned instantly to ice as they walked toward the car. Icicles also hung from Tia's fur, but she ignored them. She tottered along with Lingl and Parker as if the day were warm and she'd done nothing special.

Lingl leaned down, hugged her, and thanked her for rescuing them. Any dog towing a boat in freezing, turbulent water was hard to imagine, but a three-legged dog? A three-legged dog who actually succeeded in getting the boat to shore?

"No one will ever believe this," Lingl told Parker.

"Heaven goes by favor. If it went by merit, you would stay out and your dog would go in."

—MARK TWAIN

Annette McDonald adopted

Norman, a blond Labrador retriever puppy, on the very day before he was scheduled to be euthanized at a Seaside, Oregon, animal shelter. The pup appeared to be healthy, but when he reached the age of nine months, he began misjudging distances and bumping into doors and furniture. A veterinarian diagnosed an incurable genetic disorder that had caused his retina to deteriorate. Norman would be blind for the rest of his life.

Annette's friends watched him stumble and smash into tables and chairs. "Put him down," they urged. "He's no good to anybody."

"I'd never put him down," she retorted. "Norman is part of my family."

The dog showed great courage. Although some blind dogs become so fearful and depressed that they refuse to take one step alone, Norman seemed to accept his fate and went on with his life in his familiar house and yard. He even enjoyed going to the beach, where the wind ruffled his fur and he could smell the salt and fish in the sea air. He also managed to fetch sticks, by using senses other than sight. When Annette threw a stick for him, he followed her scent on the wood and the "thunk" of the stick hitting the sand.

One afternoon Norman lay on the beach and sniffed the air. In the distance, Lisa Nibley, a teenager, swam out into the ocean with her brother. Although she was a good swimmer, the strong current rapidly pulled her into deep water. She tried to return to shore but could not swim against the tide.

When she yelled for help, people on the beach noticed her but thought she was just playing with her brother. But Norman was alert to something frantic in the pitch and tone of Lisa's voice. He cocked his head, listened, and realized that she was in trouble. Standing up, he headed in the direction of Lisa's shouts. When the cold water hit his shoulders, he started paddling toward her.

Annette watched in amazement from the beach. She hadn't known that her dog could swim. Using Lisa's voice as a beacon, though, he swam farther and farther. Without the security of seeing where he was going, Norman focused only on getting to Lisa. He blinked against the salty waves and strained to keep his head above them. When he finally reached Lisa, she grabbed his fur and he held her up. They splashed and struggled in the waves.

Norman seemed confused about what to do next. As he circled around with Lisa hanging onto him, Annette could tell that he was trying to figure out in which direction he should swim to get to shore. To help him find his way, she shouted, "Norman! Norman!"

Following Annette's voice, he slowly towed Lisa toward the beach. But then Lisa somehow lost her grip on his fur. As she flailed her arms to keep her head above water, Norman sniffed the air and tried to locate her by scent, but that was impossible. The ocean smells drowned out any trace of Lisa.

> Annette watched in amazement from the beach. . . . Without the security of seeing where he was going, Norman focused only on getting to Lisa.

Again he circled in the water. Annette knew that he couldn't locate Lisa because he couldn't see her.

"He's blind! Call his name!" she yelled to Lisa. "His name is Norman."

"Norman!" Lisa shouted. "Norman!"

The dog swam to her as quickly as he could and with great effort towed her to shore.

"We are alone, absolutely alone on this chance planet, and,

amid all the forms of life that surround us, not one, excepting the dog,

has made an alliance with us."

—Maurice Maeterlink

Belle, a black Labrador retriever in Lunenburg, Nova Scotia, was obedient and loving. Not *once* did Belle refuse to come when called. Like a loyal guard, she protected Kenny Knickles, age three, and followed him everywhere.

"I'm going out to play," Kenny told his mother, Nancy, one winter morning.

She looked up from the newspaper at the kitchen table. "Have fun."

Belle filed out the door behind Kenny. Besides watching after him, she kicked soccer balls to him, retrieved his hockey pucks, and hauled him around the yard on a sleigh by a rope clenched in her teeth. When Belle accompanied Kenny, Nancy never worried.

She finished the newspaper and talked for a moment on the telephone, then got up to check on Kenny. He and Belle, she discovered, had left the yard. While she'd been on

the phone, they'd probably gotten cold and come back inside. Nancy searched the house, but they were both missing.

Nancy walked through the snow to the nearby woods where they usually played. She found no trace of them. When she shouted their names, Kenny did not answer. What was even more cause for alarm was that Belle did not come. Worried, Nancy hurried back home and phoned her neighbors, but no one had seen Kenny and Belle.

Panicked, Nancy telephoned her husband, Kenneth, at his office. "They *have* to be lost in the woods," she insisted.

"Did you look around the channel?" The Lunenburg Harbour Channel, which then would have been at half-tide and about ten feet deep, bordered the Knickles' property.

"They never go anywhere near the water.

"Side by Side" ~ Nigel Hemming

They can't be there," Nancy reassured Kenneth—and herself.

As Kenneth hurried home, his mind circled around all the possibilities of where his son might be and why Belle hadn't come to Nancy's call. Crossing the bridge over the channel, he glanced down into the partly frozen water and was stunned to see Belle hanging by her claws to an icy ledge along the bank. Only her head and paws were visible above the slush.

Belle could easily have let go of the bank and swum to safety. Instead, Kenneth was certain, with her black body against the white snow, that she was marking the spot where his son could be found. Hanging there, she wanted someone to see her and come to rescue Kenny. Using her body as a signal, she was calling for help.

> . . . he glanced down into the partly frozen water and was stunned to see Belle hanging by her claws to an icy ledge along the bank.

Kenneth parked the car and ran to help her, drenched and shivering, onto the bank. When he put his head into the water to look under a crust of ice for Kenny, he saw one of his son's Mickey Mouse mittens at the bottom of the channel.

Kenneth's heart beat with such force that his temples pounded. As Belle whined, he threw his hat into the water to see which direction it would float—and which direction the water might have pulled Kenny under the ice. Following the hat with his eyes, Kenneth spotted a small piece of Kenny's blue snowsuit on the channel's surface *just eight feet from where Belle had been hanging*. The boy had turned upside down in the water. Air that was trapped under his suit barely kept him afloat.

Just as Kenneth saw his son, Belle jumped back into the water and swam to save him. Nancy ran to the channel while Kenneth leaped across it from chunk to chunk of ice. Lying on a thick frozen slab to anchor him-self, he pulled Belle, then Kenny out of the water. Belle watched as Kenneth frantically pushed on Kenny's chest; water gushed out of the boy's mouth.

Kenneth picked the boy up and jumped back across floating ice cakes to shore. Certain that his son was dead, he was numb with shock. Nancy buried her face in her hands and sobbed. Belle barked as if she were calling for help.

When firemen arrived, the dog was so excited to see them that she whimpered, leaped on them, and tried to get into the ambulance with Kenny's lifeless body. As the ambulance sped away, she ran after it until Nancy and Kenneth forced her to come back home, where she paced from room to room and seemed lost and inconsolable.

Nancy and Kenneth put her in the basement and drove, grief-stricken, to the hospital. They believed that the doctors would never be able to bring Kenny back to life.

"He was in the water half an hour," a doctor told them. "If we revive him, he'll be brain dead."

Doctors tried to revive him anyway. Although they got Kenny's heart beating, they were not optimistic. Kenny, they warned, had "a five percent chance of making it."

For days as Kenny fought for his life, Kenneth and Nancy traveled back and forth to the hospital. Belle moped at home. Occasionally, she walked to the channel and looked across the water, perhaps to see if Kenny was there. She ran around the yard as if she were searching for him, then sat on the front stoop and watched the road for him.

After three weeks, he came home—without brain damage. A miracle.

Another miracle had been Belle's intelligence and sacrifice. For weeks the Knickles asked themselves, "What if? . . ." What if Belle had left Kenny in the channel and had come to Nancy's call? And what if the tide had dragged Kenny away under the ice while Belle was gone? Then, even the dog might not have known where Kenny was. If she'd not hung, wet and shivering, onto the bank to mark the spot, Kenneth never would have found his son in time.

Although Belle loved the water as much as most retrievers do, she never again swam in the channel where Kenny had almost drowned. Occasionally, she stood on the bank and barked at the water. Remembering? Warning Kenny to stay away? Still protecting him from danger? No one knew for sure.

"Histories are more full of examples of the fidelity of dogs than of friends."

—ALEXANDER POPE

Sparky, a blond Labrador retriever, had not had a good start in life. An irresponsible woman in Tullahoma, Tennessee, had bought him as a cuddly pup and then had become distressed at his eating so much and mushrooming into a hulking adolescent. She traded Sparky to a garage mechanic for a used car. The mechanic then gave him to another man, who went on vacation and left the dog with his neighbor, Bo Culbertson.

However, being shunted from place to place for a year and a half apparently had not ruined Sparky. Instead of becoming

"Fraternal Bond" ~ Nigel Hemming

insecure, the dog was loving and outgoing. In just a few days, Bo grew attached to him.

Sparky's owner came home from his trip and asked Bo, "You want the dog?"

Of course he did. Finally, Sparky had a real home where he belonged and where someone loved and appreciated him.

Sparky seemed to be grateful—and he was always hungry for both affection *and* food. He grew from eighty-five pounds to a strapping one hundred fifty. The dog was supremely loyal to Bo and slept next to him every night. Each morning, they hiked a mile together.

On one of the walks, about four hundred yards from the house, Bo suddenly felt weak and dizzy. The world around him faded to gray, then turned black. Trying to steady himself, he shoved his hand under Sparky's steel choke chain and collapsed on the road.

Sparky realized that something terrible was happening and Bo needed help. But with the man's hand tangled in his choke collar, Sparky could not free himself in order to fetch Bo's wife, Dottie. Trying to walk forward and drag Bo home would not work either because in just a few steps, the choke chain would strangle Sparky.

The dog turned around, so the chain would cut into the base of his skull and not into his throat. With the steel links pressing painfully into his flesh, Sparky *walked backwards* and pulled Bo along the road. Step by agonizing step, the dog kept tugging. His task was nearly impossible, not only because of the steel cutting into him and choking him, but also because of Bo's weighing 227 pounds.

After Sparky dragged Bo two hundred yards, he regained consciousness just enough to realize how painful the dog's efforts to get him home must be. In order to help Sparky, Bo pulled his hand out from under the choke chain and leaned his body across Sparky's back. The dog struggled the last two hundred yards home under Bo's weight—seventy-seven pounds heavier than the dog himself. Just as Dottie came outside to leave for work, she was stunned to see Sparky set Bo down at the front door.

The house was so far from the hospital that Dottie was afraid to wait for an ambulance; she could get Bo there faster if she drove him herself. But Dottie was not strong enough to carry him to the car. Once again, Sparky took Bo on his back. Straining and heaving, the dog carried him to the passenger door, where Dottie rolled him onto the front seat. She sped away and left Sparky behind, exhausted.

At the hospital, doctors discovered that the arteries to Bo's heart were blocked. Immediately he underwent triple-bypass surgery. Due to complications that required two more surgeries, Bo spent three months, close to death, in his hospital bed. For all those

> Bo suddenly felt weak and dizzy. The world around him faded to gray, then turned black. Trying to steady himself, he shoved his hand under Sparky's steel choke chain and collapsed on the road.

months, Sparky waited on Bo's empty bed at home and refused to move except to eat or go out on a leash. When Bo finally did come home and had to spend another year in bed, Sparky lay beside him constantly.

In time, one of the dog's legs became cancerous. Though in the past it had been strong enough to support Bo's weight, now the leg could barely hold up Sparky's body. He had three surgeries, but the cancer spread to his lungs. Bo had to put him down.

Bo's voice still breaks when he admits how much he misses Sparky. The dog's photograph on the wall cannot replace his fur, breath, wagging tail, and gentle presence. As do so many people who have been deeply touched by an animal, Bo hopes to meet Sparky again when he dies.

"If I pray hard enough, Sparky will be with me," he said.

With God, Bo believes, all things are possible—including a reunion with a compassionate dog who sacrificed so much for him.

"The poor dog, in life the firmest friend.

The first to welcome, foremost to defend."

—LORD BYRON

Reprinted from

THE COMPASSION OF ANIMALS ~ 1997

Parnell: Black Angel

By Jane & Michael Stern

In July 1995, a seven-week-old black Labrador Retriever named Parnell was evaluated by a team of people who are experts in canine character.

They gathered around the roly-poly being and noted his lively expression and inquisitive nature, as well as a readiness to forgive someone who held him down and restrained him several seconds against his will.

They purposely tried to scare the little puppy by snapping open an umbrella in front of his face. Parnell, who was scampering freely on a linoleum floor, skidded to a stop and cocked his head. He was curious. The testers rested the open umbrella in his path and tried to

"Little One" ~ John Silver

coax him onto its web. At first, he wanted no part of it, but soon curiosity overwhelmed apprehension. Parnell climbed on, and when the umbrella rocked underneath his weight, he froze. But his tail stayed high and his ears stayed perked and almost instantly he returned to his examination of the strange, wobbly object.

The sudden rattle of a can full of coins made the tiny creature momentarily drop his tail out of fear, but again, his curiosity drew him toward the frightening noise to sniff it out. Soon, the tail was up and wagging, fear forgotten.

Parnell was very much enjoying his test, even the scary parts. He especially was thrilled to follow after anyone who strolled briskly around the room; he delighted in chasing after a towel that one of the testers dragged along the floor; and he was totally relaxed, even quite cheerful, when someone immobilized him by picking him up—he was no more than a handful—and holding him away from their chest, straight-armed in the air, thus preventing him from continuing his explorations.

After a half hour of such scrutiny, the people testing Parnell concluded that he was bright, willing, and resilient—all good qualities. On the other hand, they noted a strong affection for people, a devotion so intense that it could develop into servility. By nature, most puppies are submissive to a degree—toward their mother or toward the humans who care for them—and Parnell's apparent willingness to please is a charming quality many people treasure in an adult pet dog. But for what this young puppy was fated to

do, a too dependent nature would have been an insurmountable handicap. A guide dog for the blind needs to lead, not follow.

Parnell was born to a life of service. Generations of his forebears were guide dogs and his father and his mother produced dozens of puppies that grew up to lead blind people through the world. . . .

The class of twelve blind people

gather in the Campbell Lounge near the dining area, finding chairs along one wall, so head trainer Kathy Zubrycki can brief them. Kathy, a handsome woman who looks like she could have been a ranch wife in Montana a hundred years ago, sits by the fireplace flanked by Jessica Sanchez and Sue McCahill, who have worked so closely with the eighteen dogs since September and have used all their knowledge and intuition to pair them up with the right people. One member of the class, jittery with anticipation, grins as the thought dawns on him: "I guess this is the ultimate blind date."

Jessica and Sue chuckle nervously; they feel the awesome responsibility of matchmaking *twelve* blind dates. Their interest in the dates' working out well goes beyond their professionalism and their desire to help the blind people. In four months of training the dogs, they have grown tremendously attached to them; they know their strengths, weaknesses, and quirks. As they taught the dogs to respond to voice commands and harness cues, they worked through a thousand potential hazards alongside them, all in the interest of exposing them to everything life might eventually throw their way. They went to crowded shopping malls where they were taught how to lead a blind person on and off an escalator, they crossed busy city streets at rush hour, they navigated over active train tracks and along narrow footpath bridges in the woods. Some of the dogs attended the ticker-tape parade for the Yankees after the World Series. Sue and Jessica are fully confident the dogs can do a good job. And they are as weepy as a pair of proud mothers who are about to watch their handsome, well-behaved young boys join the army.

"We call this phase the turnover," Kathy tells the assembled students. "These dogs have gone from their puppy homes to a kennel, from a family to a pack. Each of those transitions was traumatic in its own way. After the kennel, the instructors came into the picture, and after four months with them, the dogs have learned exactly what to expect and who will greet them every morning. Now, the dogs are being uprooted again, and we are introducing them to you. They will be confused. But the turnover works because these dogs want to please. They want to attach themselves to somebody. That somebody is going to be you. The instructors' job now is to pull away. It will take some time. But your job is an easy one. All you have to do is love them." There is a long, silent pause as Kathy lets this thought sink in.

Kathy explains that when the students are introduced to their dogs, everything should be low-key. "Don't try any commands at all. No roughhousing, no discipline. For the first couple of days, *we* will be the bad guys. We will do all the corrections. All you have to do is bond."

As she speaks, several of the dogs play outside on the lawn, chasing each other and running after balls tossed by assistant trainers. But the glass on the sliding doors is thick enough so the students cannot hear anything; nor, of course, can they see. Their dogs are still a mystery to them. And the dogs themselves have no reason to expect that they are about to meet their partners and embark on a whole new life.

Before the actual transfer of the dogs, some of the anxiety in the Campbell Lounge

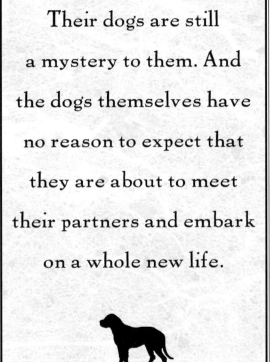

Their dogs are still a mystery to them. And the dogs themselves have no reason to expect that they are about to meet their partners and embark on a whole new life.

"All in the Family" ~ Nigel Hemming

is lessened by playing a little game that lets the students know their dog's name.

Addressing Murry Dimon, a kindly retread from West Seneca, New York, Kathy says, "Your dog is a black lab, male, whose name sounds like the man who parted the red sea. . . ."

"Is it Moses?" Murry queries.

"It's Moseley!" Sue bursts out. Of all the dogs they have trained, Moseley is a special favorite with Sue and Jessica. A gift to the program rather than a product of the breeding colony, Moseley is one of those magical creatures with an expression of kindness, deep sympathy, and intelligence. *Big sweet pup* were the words used to characterize him at his seven-week evaluation test, a description that still fits, even though he has become a responsible and well-trained adult dog.

Craig Hedgecock, a massively muscular young man with top ranking among collegiate wrestlers in the east, is getting his first dog. "There is a company that delivers things called Wells *blank*," Kathy says to him. "But replace the *F* with a *V*."

"Vargo?" Craig wonders.

"Yes!" says Sue, who trained Vargo.

"Vargo," Craig repeats to himself. "What a cool name!"

"Esther, on Broadway there is a show called *blank Victoria*. He is a yellow lab."

"His name is Victor!" student Esther Acha calls out with glee.

When Bob Serrano is told that his dog is a yellow lab named Eagle, he says with wonder, "I dreamt of a yellow lab!"

"Linette, do you know *Star Trek?*" Kathy asks.

Linette Stevens, back for her third dog, is a woman with a birth defect that makes her as diminutive as a small child, and with a child's voice. She says she knows the TV show quite well. Many of the quiz-show questions demand a knowledge of visible popular culture, with which these active blind people seem at least as familiar as are any sighted folk. Even those who have been blind since birth seem to have absorbed a familiarity with icons that most of us think of as primarily visual.

"The main character on *Star Trek* was named Captain *blank*."

"Oh, my God!" Linette says, laughing with surprise. "My best friend's name is Kirk! How will he know who I'm calling?" Later, Linette tells us that her buddy Kirk also is blind, but additionally suffers from a severe equilibrium problem. His dog, specially trained by Kathy's husband, Ted, is one of those that serves not only as a visual guide, but as an aid to maintaining balance.

Kathy comes to Cindy Blair. "Cindy, do you remember the show *Bonanza?*"

Cindy nods, intensely curious as to where Kathy is going with this line of questioning.

"What was the name of the actor who played the oldest brother?"

"Hoss?" someone else volunteers.

"No," Kathy says. "It was *blank* Roberts."

"Pernell?" Cindy guesses.

"Parnell!" Kathy says.

"Parnell," Cindy says. She beams with the joy of knowing. "Parnell," she repeats quietly to herself. As the game continues, Cindy mouths the word *Parnell* over and over, grinning to herself.

When the game is done and everybody knows the names of their dogs, Kathy jokes, "Those of you who don't want your dogs, stay here. The rest of you—anybody who wants to meet their dog—leave the room and we will call you back one by one." As fast as twelve blind people can hurry out of an unfamiliar room into the unknown hallways of the school, the students exit the Campbell Lounge. Several feel their way to a small recreation cubicle set aside for smokers, where they light up and puff deeply. Others mill in the hallway, waiting for their names to be called.

Each student is called back by Sue or Jessica over the school's loudspeaker system. The extreme tension of meeting one's partner is almost unbearable, not only among the students but especially among Sue, Jessica, and Kathy, who know perhaps even better than the novices just how important a guide dog can become to its master. To defuse the anxiety, their loudspeaker announcements are whimsical, silly, or overly romantic.

"Spencer, oh, Spencer, there is someone waiting for you in the Campbell Lounge,"

> The extreme tension of meeting one's partner is almost unbearable . . . especially among Sue, Jessica, and Kathy, who know . . . just how important a guide dog can become to its master.

Jessica croons. "Please come meet him. Bring your leash . . ., but don't bring your cane."

"Hi," says Sue over the speaker. "My name is Vargo. I am waiting for Craig in the Campbell Lounge."

Craig sits in a chair at one side of the large room while Sue holds Vargo, a male German Shepherd, on the other side of the room. Sue stands and gives Vargo his command to move forward. Jessica, standing near Craig, is the dog's target, but with subtle body language and unseen cues, the two trainers direct Vargo directly into Craig. Craig is leaning off the edge of the chair, and when abruptly he feels the dog's warm breath in front of his face, he slips off the seat to the floor. The big wrestler is weak with the emotion he feels as Vargo, wriggling with doggy joy, licks him all over his face.

"He has a soft, sensitive eye," Sue says. "He has a white cross on his chest."

Craig is on the floor intertwined with Vargo. He is laughing and crying at the same time. He manages to croak out, "I'm all broken up" as he tousles with the happy dog.

Sue guides his hands to clip a leash onto Vargo's collar and helps the two of them walk out of the room together, side by side.

"I'm a-comin', I'm a-comin'," calls Alison

"Guiding Lights" ~ Nigel Hemming

Dolan from the hallway when her name is announced and she is summoned in to meet her dog Colleen.

"She is blond like you," Sue tells Alison. "Her belly is almost white. She has the biggest, roundest eyes." Alison hugs her little yellow lab, tears streaming down her face. She straightens up and feels for Colleen's collar, then clips on her leash. As the two walk out together, Sue is radiant with pride. This appears to be a perfect match. She cannot help but exclaim, "You look so good together already!"

Even before Murry Dimon is called in to meet Moseley, Jessica Sanchez is fighting back tears. "This is going to get messy," she says. "Moseley is so special. He is a dog who would die for you. He makes you laugh. No matter how bad you feel, he can take care of you." When he meets Murry, Moseley fairly attacks his new master with affection, mussing his neat comb-over hairdo hair with a wet nose so the hair stands up on one side of his head like a furry tidal wave. Moseley licks Murry all over his face. Murry is at first taken aback by the overload of affection, but soon he melts off his chair to the floor and puts his arms in a big hug around Moseley's neck. He tries to say something, but words fail him. He stands, trying to straighten his clothes and using his fingers to comb his mussed hair back. Emotional by nature, Jessica is also speechless, sobbing silently as she watches her favorite dog walk out the door. "He looks good on you, Kathy calls to Murry, finally breaking the silence.

Overwhelmed by emotions, Jessica is falling apart. "Oh, this is horrible," she mutters between Kleenex-muffled sniffles, barely able to regain her composure when it comes time to call Cindy Blair into the lounge. As Cindy enters, Jessica, Sue, and Kathy all sing "Happy Birthday" to her. Cindy's shallow breath is short from anticipation. She sits on the edge of a chair, aware that her new dog, Parnell, is at the opposite side of the room.

"Call him," Sue says.

"He'll come to you," says Jessica, who is holding him by the collar.

"Parnell . . . " Cindy is so short of breath that she calls his name quietly. He hears, but Jessica is still holding him. Cindy knows she has to muster more energy. "Parnell!" she calls out. Jessica lets go of the dog and Parnell lopes across the room into Cindy's arms. She hugs him and kisses him as he licks her face. "He's small," she says, her practiced hands running up and down his body. "Is he small?" The instructors don't answer. Most physical details are kept in abeyance at first meeting, the idea being to encourage students to create an image of their dog based on touch,

> This appears to be a perfect match . . . "You look so good together already!"

feel, and actual contact rather than statistics. They also don't want to encourage inevitable comparisons: *my dog is bigger than your dog.*

"Oh, thank you," Cindy says, "Thank you, thank you, thank you." Jessica helps her walk out of the room and comes back looking like she needs a transfusion. The emotions of the afternoon have drained her. The ends of her long brown hair are wet with tears. Is it this emotional with every class? The three trainers nod, too spent to speak.

❦ Parnell: Going Home ❦

The day after the graduation ceremony at Guiding Eyes for the Blind in Yorktown Heights, retreads go home. Novice dog owners remain at the school another week for additional training to help them cope with whatever unique situations their lives might present their dog: plane travel, crowds, hours of patient inactivity while their master doesn't need guiding. Those who have never owned a dog must be taught certain basic routines that every good pet owner needs to know: grooming (minimal for Labrador Retrievers), regular health checks, and food preferences.

Even those blind people who are familiar with pet care need to be reminded of the difference between a pet and a working dog. Guide dogs have been programmed to thrive on a fairly regimented life: feedings at a regular hour, predictable periods of R&R, and a high expectation of responsible behavior. When students take new dogs home, they are told not to let any other family member play with it, walk it, or give it orders, at least at first. Their primary goal should be to get the dog to focus entirely on them, not anyone else. It is furthermore expected that at least for the first few weeks the dog should spend the night in its master's bedroom on a tie-down (as it did at the school). This minimizes wandering and household accidents, and further reinforces the lifeline connection between dog and master. Later, when the tie-down is eliminated and the dog is given run of the house, a majority of guide dogs choose to make their special place a spot in the master's bedroom.

For retread Cindy Blair and her new dog, Parnell, a trip home means seven hours on the train. "My husband informed me that because I was coming home on Superbowl Sunday, I'd have to take a cab from the station," Cindy laughs. "But I do look forward to the train ride. That is seven hours' bonding time for me and the Parnster."

Cindy carefully orchestrates Parnell's arrival Sunday night. Although she knows that she and only she should be with Parnell during these first moments of their togetherness at home, she hands Parnell's leash to her husband before she even gets to the front door so he can take the new dog into the backyard and play with him there. Cindy has Brent's feelings to think about. She doesn't want to walk into the house after a month away and have Brent see her in the company of another, younger dog. So when she enters, she enters alone. Brent sniffs and licks her and wags his tail with joy. After she and her old guide say a long hello, she tells him, "Brent, I want you to come meet your new friend." She leads the veteran to the doors that open into the backyard. Parnell enters, curious and cautious. The two dogs—both professionals well trained to deal with any circumstances—give each other a good once-over, then relax and sit side by side at Cindy's feet, waiting to work.

Later that night, Parnell is allowed to explore the house at his leisure. At bedtime, the two dogs sleep on either side of the bed in the master bedroom.

Monday morning at eight o'clock, Brent whines when the harness comes out and Cindy doesn't put it on him. He pushes his way close to her, sitting obediently at her feet. But all he can do is watch her put the harness on Parnell and walk out the door with her new guide. As she swiftly moves along the sidewalk toward the bus stop, Cindy herself is crying.

She boards the bus and Parnell guides her into downtown Rochester for coffee with a friend. Parnell takes her into a big office building, across busy streets, into elevators and up and down escalators. "It is like we've been a team for years," Cindy declares. "It is like he just slid into my life. And he fits perfectly." When her friends meet him, they comment on how good he looks paired with her: both dog and master are dapper characters with a bouyant mien, and he soon begins to sport a bandanna to match what she is wearing when they go out on the town.

Parnell is flawless his first day on the job, but Cindy makes one mistake. She was so thrilled to have her new dog that when she left her house in the morning, she did not landmark it—a basic technique of stopping and pulling on the harness a few times to let a dog know that this is a significant destination, a place to stop or turn. So when she and Parnell return from town, the diligent guide dog walks right past her house and continues moving forward, having no sense yet of where he lives. By the end of the block, Cindy realizes that Parnell will continue walking forever. He needs her to tell him where to turn in. So she directs him back to the place he will soon know as home. That night, she calls her friends at Guiding Eyes—the first-timers who had stayed for an extra week of training—and warns them, "Whatever you do when you get home, landmark your house!"

The next day, Cindy landmarks the crossing at the nearby railroad tracks, and the day after that she takes him to her son's school, where she has PTA business to attend to. Parnell's upbringing at Johns Hopkins serves him well. He is entirely comfortable negotiating hallways and classrooms.

One morning well into Parnell's tenure as her guide dog, Cindy clips on the harness and walks outside. About two houses down, she begins to feel that something is wrong.

146

"Generations" ~ Nigel Hemming

Parnell isn't going well at all. He is pulling and tugging. Then Cindy realizes what has happened. She has put the harness on Brent rather than on Parnell, and Brent once again is flinching when her cues gall his tender skin. Somehow, that old dog managed to figure out a way to get Parnell far from the front door where he normally waits when he knows

Cindy is going out. "Brent didn't say a thing when I put the harness on him, just the way I used to do," Cindy says. "He knew he had me fooled." Later, she buys a different collar for Brent so she can feel who's who and Brent can never play that trick again.

Still, Brent always waits by the door, hoping against hope that this time Cindy will take him out into the world and let him be her eyes instead of the young newcomer. But Brent's days in a harness are definitely over. Not that there aren't good compensations for being retired.

Parnell, the working dog, is never allowed on the furniture. Brent can sleep in bed. "That is a privilege of his retirement," Cindy proclaims. "But once he got used to it, he started gloating by hanging his head over the side of the bed and lording his status over Parnell. That's not fair, so now he is not allowed to hang off the side where Parnell can see him."

As Parnell has settled into his work life, the Blair family has come to know new facets of his personality. "It took me some time to realize how much Parnell likes to play," Cindy says. "He is so good at his work, but he likes his fun, too." One of his great pleasures, they have discovered, is dancing. Cindy's fifteen-year-old son Michael kneels down so Parnell can put both paws on his

Daniel

shoulders. Parnell kisses Michael, who then stands up and waltzes around the room, paw-in-arm with the happy black lab.

At home, when he is not in his harness, Parnell doesn't go anywhere without his Stuffy toy—a sort of gingerbread man with sheep fleece. He carries it around with him and he sleeps with it. "Oh, how he hates it when I clean that toy," Cindy says. "He sits by the dryer waiting for it to come out. And the first thing he does, when it is still warm, is to rub it all around on the floor so it gets dirty again. We recently bought two backup Stuffies just in case something happens to this one. We're going to do everything we can to see to it that Parnell is happy. He deserves it."

When the Blairs open their backyard pool, it becomes apparent that Parnell yearns to go swimming. Of course he does—water is many labs' favorite element; and Cindy recalls Susan Fisher-Owens' story of Parnell putting his head in the spray from the fire hydrant when he was a pup. But because it is an above-ground pool, the Blairs worry that an errant claw could tear the sides and flood

their yard. So Parnell gets his own pool: a little "Mr. Turtle" wading tub designed for children, complete with floating rubber balls and inflatable boat. He is in ecstasy; and every morning when he goes into the backyard at 6 A.M., his first order of business is to find the garden hose and drag it to the pool, hinting to his family that he'd like it filled.

Parnell learns to relish watching baseball. At young Michael's encouragement, Cindy and Parnell join him at day games played in Rochester's minor league stadium where, Cindy boasts, "The handicapped seats are the best!" Sitting with Cindy and Michael just above the boxes between home plate and first base, Parnell watches every move on the field. Teenage Michael is especially pleased with the dog's company, at the ball game and elsewhere around town, because he soon discovers that the handsome, brown-eyed, eighty-seven-pound hunk is what he calls a chick magnet. "Beautiful girls are always stopping by to pet the nice dog," Cindy says. "Parnell has something women can't resist—and I confirmed this with the Fisher-Owenses, who said he

> Parnell learns to relish watching baseball . . . Sitting with Cindy and Michael just above the boxes between home plate and first base, Parnell watches every move on the field.

149

always was a ladies' man—so my son sits there and gives them permission to pet *his* dog. 'Mom,' he whispers, 'Move aside.'"

Cindy is most amazed by The Parn Man's strict adherence to the rules as he has learned them. Off-duty, he loves to splash gaily in his pool and even to coax some play from Brent (whom he still respects as the senior dog around the house), but when Parnell is in harness, nothing can distract him or weaken his resolve to do his job. If Cindy is with a group of people and the others jay-walk across the street, Parnell refuses to follow. Instead, he leads Cindy to the crosswalk. "He will not take a shortcut," Cindy says. "So it might take me a few extra minutes to get somewhere, but I don't mind because I know I am safe. I have gone farther with him than with any other dog, so far that my family bought me a cell phone to keep in touch. Parnell has such an incredible sense of duty that I have never once had to discipline him. He is too good to be true. Sometimes, I wait for that other paw to fall . . . but I don't believe it ever will."

Cindy comes to believe fully in Parnell on Easter Sunday. That day, the two of them go to church early in the morning for a children's breakfast party. A sixteen-year-old friend of Cindy's son Michael is playing the part of the Easter Bunny, outfitted in a full body costume with big ears, floppy feet, and pompom tail. Parnell knows the boy well, but when he sees a six-foot-tall bunny saunter into the room, ears up and whiskers akimbo, he is flabbergasted. No experiences he had during his Guiding Eyes education quite prepared him for an encounter with a gigantic rodent that moves like a man. Parnell backs up and barks, a natural reaction in any animal confronted by a big, scary alien. But he doesn't run, nor does he attack. After a short stand-off between gigantic rabbit and dog, Parnell's well-honed instincts steady him; months of expert training offer further reassurance. Just as he did when he was seven weeks old and overcame his shock at the snapped-opened umbrella and the rattling can full of coins, just as he did when Russ Post shot the .32 pistol in the air at the In-For-Training tests, Parnell assesses the situation and decides he can deal with it. Panic fading, he cautiously approaches the huge rabbit; and finally, when he is close enough for a good sniff, he gets the nice, reassuring scent of the boy he knows. His tail wags. He can relax because he is safe . . . and because he knows his Cindy is safe, too.

Reprinted from

TWO PUPPIES ~ 1998

"Let's Play Ball" ~ Michael Jackson

"A really companionable and indispensable dog is an accident of nature. You can't

get it by breeding for it, and you can't buy it with money. It just happens along."

—E. B. WHITE, *The Care and Training of a Dog*

Let's Go Huntin'

By Bill Tarrant

Calendars of Our Joy

I sit on the porch as the sun works west and think of the dogs that have led me, and abided me, through a long life afield. Through the slant of the sun, in the shadow of the trees, coming up the gravel drive—I see them now. Old gun dogs that have stood the test of time and event and circumstance. They come now, slowly, and lay at foot or close to side, jowls flat, eyes faded with the fog of cataract, their muzzles and paws white or speckled salt and pepper. But they come. They want to be close—as they always did.

They are great treasures, these old dogs. For they are more than themselves lying there. They are us. Parts of us. A hill climbed together

"Wish You Were Here" ~ Nigel Hemming

and the crimson leaves of sumac danced in the morning sunlight. The well looked in and the rock dropped and the chill of the dark hole seemed forever before the splash was heard.

They are sweaty palms, for you were hosting your boss and he'd never gunned over a trained dog before; yet Pup was so birdy you couldn't be sure he'd hold for wing and shot.

They are the iced mace of wind thrown by bad-dad winter, off to the north, blowing the redleg mallards off their last haunts. Blowing them south, flying like buckshot. And you're gripping Pup and whispering, "No head up," as you fit the duck call to your lips. But it is cold and you know it will freeze to the skin. But you call. And the lead hen throws her body high, looking down and back, seeing the iced-in blocks pointing bill-up to the slate sky.

And now they come, shingles ripped loose from some old barn, and the wind is driving them crazily toward your decoys and you stand and the old gun barks and the dog launches. He's breaking ice and standing high in the water, though his feet don't touch bottom. And you wish you'd never shot.

> And you take the duck and the dog shivers . . . You entered nature and went duck hunting and tricked the wild fowl to your trap and the dog closed the door.

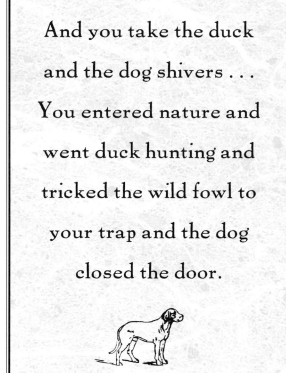

For nothing can live out there. Not even Pup in the prime of his life. Yet he clomps the big bright drake and spins about, throwing water with his whipping tail. He comes for you—swimming, by instinct, for the drake covers his face.

And you're out of the blind now and running the bank, yelling out. And the retriever comes to shore, not stopping to shake, and heads straight for you. But the black dog turns instantly silver. The water has frozen that fast. And you take the duck and the dog shivers, his teeth chattering, and the pelvic-drive muscles convulse. Then he spins in the tall yellow grass—he runs and rubs the side of his jowls in the mud and stubble.

No duck is worth this—remember saying that?—and the two of you go back to the house. Back to the towel you rub Pup with and the fire you sit before, and the wind makes a harmonica of your house-siding and whomps down the fireplace to billow the ashes.

But the duck does lay on the sideboard by the sink. You entered nature and went duck hunting and tricked the wild fowl to your trap and the dog closed the door.

Still, you're sorry you went; but years later, when the smell of that day's wet fur is forgotten and even the curled tailfeathers from the mallard have long been blown from the fireplace mantle, you'll remember—you'll remember that retrieve and old Pup will come to side and you'll fondle his ears and the memory of that cold day and that single duck will become the most important thing that ever happened in your life.

For Pup is dying.

And you can't see him that you don't have to smile and call him to you. It may be the last time you ever touch his ear. But that's just part of it. You're dying, too. Pup will just go first. As he always went first in the field or at the blind. You followed him, not the other way around. It was he who entered the unknown and learned its bareness or its bounty.

And you love the old dog, for he lived your life. He was the calendar of your joy. Why, you could leap the stream when you got your first pup. Remember? And you could hunt all day. Cold? Bosh! And the apple in your pocket was all it took to fuel you from Perkins' fence to Hadley's barn—a limit of bobwhite later.

But now the arthritis hobbles you. And the cold. It seems to come and sit in your bones like an unwanted stranger.

So you don't just call Pup to side, you call your life. You run your fingers through your past when you fondle his ears.

And you stand and go to the gun case. Why, the bluing's gone from that old Superpose. Then you remember when you bought it—long before Pup ever came into your life. And look at that duck call. There's no varnish left on the barrel. And the barrel is cracked! And the string that holds it—it was a country store back in the hills and you stopped for a loaf of bread to feed Pup. And the duck call was in your pocket, just out of its cardboard box. And you asked the proprietor for a piece of string, and he went to the meat counter and drew off a yard of it. You were always going to get a bona fide, braided lanyard.

But that's like life. You were always going to . . . .

And there's Pup. He was not a going to. He was a was. Not a put-off till tomorrow. Pup was planned and bought and trained and taken to field. That happened. And the million dollars was never made, and you never became branch manager, and your kids didn't make it through college. But Pup did all you imagined for him.

Pup was your one success.

And he is dying.

How many pups ago was it your sweater fitted loose on your belly and your belly was hard like the barrel of a cannon? But look at the sweater now. Stretched tight and tattered and faded. Why do you still wear it? There are Christmas sweaters still in their boxes, on the shelf in the closet.

And the boots. Remember? They had to be just so. But look at them now. Toes out, scuffed, heels run over. And yet you shuffle about in them.

Is it because you're holding on to the past? Is it because looking back down the road means more than looking on up ahead?

Is it because the birds you went with Pup to get were got? And now? What do they say? A bird in the hand is worth more than two. . . . Maybe that's it. Pup made you a bird-in-the-hand man.

The Royal Flush

It had snowed the night before, and you and Pup had crawled under the barbed wire fence to enter the apple orchard. The tree limbs were naked and bleak and your breath rose before you—the white of steam. Then Pup, while making a back-cast, went in point mid-air and twirled and came down contorted so his left leg stuck out with that foot barely touching the snow. You passed him, acknowledging his point, and up they came. It was a bright, new 20-gauge Franchi automatic you carried, made partly of aluminum so it was supposed to be lightning fast, and you always dreamed of the day you'd take five on the rise—the magazine was legally loaded. And up they came, and the gun stabbed at your shoulder and the smoke mingled with the steam of your breath and neither you nor Pup could believe the falling. But they were down: five bobwhite. *A royal flush.* And Pup had to be convinced to go get number four and number five. For you had never shot that many birds at one time before.

Yes. Others in those days may have been two-birds-in-the-bush hopefuls. But you and Pup did it. You went. No sunshine patriots then. No sir. The five birds lay in hand, and the snow started falling again.

He's got bad teeth now, you know? Pup has. And let's admit it. His breath stinks. And look at him, great blotches of hair stand here and there like some derelict mountain sheep that's taken to roadside begging at a national park. And he does little but sleep—he does lots of that.

There are pups to be bought, you know? Why, ads are everywhere. And some say gun dogs have gotten better than ever. Or at least the training methods have gotten so sharp you can even bring a mediocre pup along.

But no. It's always been you and Pup. And you'll wait till he's no more. But have you ever wondered? What will you be when he's gone? If he were the best part of your days, then what will there be when he's dead and buried? What will there be of you? Some grumpy old mumbler who sits by the fire and harrumphs at those come to be kind?

He's by the Gate

No, not at all. For you were a gun dog man and you went to field. Your Pup was the best gun dog you ever saw. And you watched the flash of the great black Lab as he leaped through bramble and you saw him once atop the hill—how far away was he on that cast? A half mile? And all you must do is close your eyes or, better yet, just go to the window and watch the falling leaves. Pup's out there. He's by the gate, see him? And he's leaping that way he always did, urging you to get on with it. And he darts now, to the field, and sniffs the passing mice, the dickey birds.

"In Retirement" ~ Nigel Hemming

And then you're with him, the weight of the gun reassuring in your grasp, and your stride is strong and the wind bites your cheek but you laugh and blow the white steam of cold. Always you can do this, just standing at the window—for you did this.

What of that smell of straw at the old duck blind and pouring the coffee from the thermos. Then learning how to pour the coffee from the steel cup so you could put the cup to your lips. And you never knew why the pouring made the cup manageable.

And the pride in your decoys, watching them run to the end of their cords and spinning about, ducking their heads and bobbing to drip water from their bills.

And off to the left, in that stand of multiflora rose. Hear him! The cock pheasant *car-runks*. Bright as brass he is. And you could heel Pup out of the duck blind and go get him, but you like the bird's sass. You like his arrogance. And anything that gaudy can live out there in the back of your place.

And what of that morning you and Pup were sitting there? Duck hunting—for you—didn't mean shooting ducks. It meant being there. Hearing the rustle of your heavy canvas pants and the tinkle of the dog whistles and duck calls as they danced on your chest. Blowing in cupped hands, beating them against the sides of your chest. And standing and stomping on the wood pallets you brought in, for the water rose with the late rains. And yet for that moment you and Pup were silent, and the redtailed hawk landed, right above both of you, on a bare limb.

And you were ornery. Jumped up you did and yelled, "Hey hawk!" And the hawk was so startled he hurled himself to the air with a great squawk and left a white stream all over your blind as he beat his departure. But it was still funny and you sat in the draping of hawk feces—and laughed.

Not another single living thing had that moment but you and Pup and the hawk. And the three of you made that moment momentous forever. Now the hawk is gone and Pup is going, but that moment makes you all vibrant and alive. And in a way it makes you important. How few people have an exclusive moment?

And if Pup had not taken you to field you'd not have had it. So he lies there now, that generator of meaning and memory. That's what a gun dog comes to be for us. An enricher of life. Something to take ordinary moments and make them miraculous.

Reprinted from

TARRANT TRAINS GUN DOGS ~ 1989

"Black Lab and Spaniel" ~ Nigel Hemming

In Praise of Labs—Reprint Acknowledgements

Earl of Malmsbury. 1994. "The Little Newfoundler" from *Labrador Quarterly/The Best of the First Ten Years* of the Ladrador Quarterly. Reprint, Hofflin Publishing.

Hill, Gene. 1986. "The XVth Day" from *Field & Stream*, vol. 91 (Nov. '86). Requested permission from Field & Stream.

Herriot, James. 1986. "The Dustbin Dog" from *James Herriot's Dog Stories*. Requested permission from St. Martin's Press.

Coren, Stanley. 1994. "Shotgun" from *The Intelligence of Dogs: Canine Consciousness and Capabilities*. Reprinted by permission of The Free Press, a Division of Simon & Schuster.

Hill, Gene. 1986. "It's A Dog's Life" from *Field & Stream* , vol. 98 (June '93). Requested permission from Field & Stream.

Miller, Jr. O. Victor. 1998. "Dove Tactics for the Morally Depraved and the Ethically Bankrupt" from *Georgia Sportsman & Albany Magazine*. Reprinted by permission of the author.

Paulsen, Gary. 1998. "Ike a Good Friend" from *My Life in Dog Years*. Reprinted by permission of the author.

Zern, Ed. 1984. "Exit Laughing" from *Field & Stream*, vol. 89 (October 1984). Requested permission from Field & Stream.

Mathewson, Worth. "Guest Shot: May" from *Field & Stream*, vol. 101 (May 1996). Reprinted by permission of the author.

Fergus, Jim. 1997. "Sweetz's Off-Season" from *Outdoor Life* , vol. 199 (Feb. 1998). Requested permission from Outdoor Life.

Miller, Jr. O. Victor. 1998. "Hot Grits and Blue Yonder" from *Georgia Sportsman & Albany Magazine*. Reprinted by permission of the author.

Busch, Frederick. 1995. "Gus and Dinah" from *Dog People*. Requested permission from Artisan/Workman.

Jones, Robert F. "Tale of a Pup" from *Sports Illustrated*, vol. 73, (12/31/90 - 1/7/91). Reprinted by permission of Sports Illustrated. Copyright © 1990, Time Inc.

von Kreisler, Kristin. "Labs to the Rescue" from *The Compassion of Animals: True Stories of Animal Courage and Kindness*. Reprinted by permission of Prima Publishing.

Stern, Jane & Michael. "Parnell: Black Angel" and "Parnell: Going Home" from *Two Puppies*. Requested permission from Scribner, New York.

Tarrant, Bill. 1989. "Let's Go Huntin'" from *Tarrant Trains Gun Dogs*. Reprinted by permission of Stackpole Books.

We have made every effort to determine original sources and locate copyright holders of the excerpts in this book. Grateful acknowledgement is made to the writers, publishers, and agencies listed for permission to reprint material copyrighted or controlled by them. Please bring to our attention any errors of fact, omission, or copyright.